Walker's Appeal
and
Garnet's Address

to the Slaves of the
United States of America

PUBLISHED BY JAMES C. WINSTON PUBLISHING COMPANY, INC.
Nashville, Tennessee 37205

ISBN: 1-55523-540-9

Printed in the United States of America

Francis Jackson Garrison.

125 Highland St.,

Roxbury

1888.

WALKER'S

APPEAL,

With a Brief Sketch of his Life.

BY

HENRY HIGHLAND GARNET.

AND ALSO

GARNET'S ADDRESS

TO THE SLAVES OF THE UNITED STATES OF AMERICA.

———•———

NEW-YORK:
Printed by J. H. Tobitt, 9 Spruce-st
1848.

PREFACE.

Such is the very high esteem which is entertained for the memory of DAVID WALKER, and so general is the desire to preserve his "Appeal," that the subscriber has undertaken, and performed the task of re-publication, with a brief notice of his life, having procured permission from his widow, **Mrs. Dewson.**

The work is valuable, because it was among the first, and was actually the boldest and most direct appeal in behalf of freedom, which was made in the early part of the Anti-Slavery Reformation. When the history of the emancipation of the bondmen of America shall be written, whatever name shall be placed first on the list of heroes, that of the author of the Appeal will not be second.

Troy, N. Y., April 12, 1848.

A BRIEF SKETCH

LIFE AND CHARACTER OF DAVID WALKER.

———◆———

It is generally the desire of the reader of any intellectual production, to know something of the character and the life of the author. The character of *David Wa kr* is indicated in his writings. In regard to his life, but a few materials can be gathered; but what is known of him, furnishes proof to the opinion which the friends of man have formed of him—that he possessed a noble and a courageous spirit, and that he was ardently attached to the cause of liberty.

Mr. Walker was born in Wilmington, North Carolina, Sept. 28, 1785. His mother was a free woman, and his father was a slave. His innate hatred to slavery was very early developed. When yet a boy, he declared that the slaveholding South was not the place for him. His soul became so indignant at the wrongs which his father and his kindred bore, that he determined to find some portion of his country where he would see less to harrow up his soul. Said he, "If I remain in this bloody land, I will not live long. As true as God reigns, I will be avenged for the sorrow which my people have suffered. This is not the place for me—no, no. I must leave this part of the country. It will be a great trial for me to live on the same soil where so many men are in slavery; certainly I cannot remain where I must hear their chains continually, and where I must encounter the insults of their hypocritical enslavers. Go, I must."

The youthful Walker embraced his mother, and received a mother's blessings, and turned his back upon North Carolina.

His father died a few months before his birth ; and it is a remarkable coincidence, that the son of the subject of this Memoir, was a posthumous child.

After leaving home, David Walker travelled rapidly towards the North, shaking off the dust of his feet, and breathing curses upon the system of human slavery, America's darling institution. As might be expected, he met with trials during his journey ; and at last he reached Boston, Mass., where he took up his permanent residence. There he applied himself to study, and soon learned to read and write, in order that he might contribute something to the cause of humanity. Mr. Walker, like most of reformers, was a poor man—he lived poor, and died poor.

In 1827 he entered into the clothing business in Brattle street, in which he prospered ; and had it not been for his great liberality and hospitality, he would have become wealthy. In 1828, he married Miss Eliza ————. He was emphatically a self-made man, and he spent all his leisure moments in the cultivation of his mind. Before the Anti-Slavery Reformation had assumed a form, he was ardently engaged in the work. His hands were always open to contribute to the wants of the fugitive. His house was the shelter and the home of the poor and needy. Mr. Walker is known principally by his "APPEAL," but it was in his private walks, and by his unceasing labors in the cause of freedom, that he has made his memory sacred.

With an overflowing heart, he published his "Appeal" in 1829. This little book produced more commotion among slaveholders than any volume of its size that was ever issued from an American press. They saw that it was a bold attack upon their idolatry, and that too by a black man who once lived among them. It was merely a smooth stone which this David took up, yet it terrified a host of Goliaths. When the fame of this book reached the South, the poor, cowardly, pusillanimous tyrants, grew pale behind their cotton bags, and armed themselves to the teeth. They set watches to look after their happy and contented slaves. The Governor of GEORGIA wrote to the Hon. Harrison Grey Otis, the Mayor of Boston, requesting him to suppress the Appeal. His Honor replied to the Southern Censor, that he had no power nor disposition to hinder Mr. Walker from pursuing a lawful course in the utterance of his thoughts. A company of Georgia men then bound themselves by an oath, that they would eat as little as possible until they had killed the youthful author. They also offered a reward of a thousand dollars for his head, and ten times as much for the live Walker. His consort, with the solicitude of an affectionate wife, together with some friends, advised him to go to Canada, lest he should be abducted. Walker said that he had nothing to fear from such a pack of coward blood-hounds; but if he did go, he would hurl back such thunder across the great lakes, that would cause them to tremble in their strong holds. Said he, " I will stand my ground. *Somebody must die in this cause.* I may be doomed to the stake and the fire, or to the scaffold tree, but it is not in me to falter if I can promote the work of emancipation." He did not leave the country, but was soon laid in the grave. It was the opinion of many that he was hurried out of life by the means of poison, but whether this was the case or not, the writer is not prepared to affirm.

He had many enemies, and not a few were his brethren whose cause he espoused. They said that he went too far, and was making trouble. So the Jews spoke of Moses. They valued the flesh-pots of Egypt more than the milk and honey of Canaan. He died 1830 in Bridge street, at the hopeful and enthusiastic age of 34 years. His ruling passion blazed up in the hour of death, and threw an indescribable grandeur over the last dark scene. The heroic young man passed away without a struggle, and a few weeping friends

" Saw in death his eyelids close,
Calmly, as to a night's repose,
Like flowers at set of sun."

The personal appearance of Mr. Walker was prepossessing, being six feet in height, slender and well proportioned. His hair was loose, and his complexion was dark. His son, the only child he left, is now 18 years of age, and is said to resemble his father ; he now resides at Charlestown, Mass., with his mother, Mrs. Dewson. Mr. Walker was a faithful member of the Methodist Church at Boston, whose pastor is the venerable father Snowden.

The reader thus has a brief notice of the life and character of David Walker.

WALKER'S

APPEAL,

IN FOUR ARTICLES,

TOGETHER WITH

A PREAMBLE,

TO THE

COLORED CITIZENS OF THE WORLD,

BUT IN PARTICULAR, AND VERY EXPRESSLY TO THOSE OF THE

UNITED STATES OF AMERICA.

Written in Boston, in the State of Massachusetts, Sept. 28, 1829.

SECOND EDITION, WITH CORRECTIONS, &c.

BY DAVID WALKER.

1830.

APPEAL, &c.

PREAMBLE.

My dearly beloved Brethren and Fellow Citizens :

Having travelled over a considerable portion of these United States, and having, in the course of my travels taken the most accurate observations of things as they exist—the result of my observations has warranted the full and unshakened conviction, that we, (colored people of these United States) are the most degraded, wretched, and abject set of beings that ever lived since the world began, and I pray God, that none like us ever may live again until time shall be no more. They tell us of the Israelites in Egypt, the Helots in Sparta, and of the Roman Slaves, which last, were made up from almost every nation under heaven, whose sufferings under those ancient and heathen nations were, in comparison with ours, under this enlightened and christian nation, no more than a cypher—or in other words, those heathen nations of antiquity, had but little more among them than the name and form of slavery, while wretchedness and endless miseries were reserved, apparently in a phial, to be poured out upon our fathers, ourselves and our children by *christian* Americans !

These positions, I shall endeavour, by the help of the Lord, to demonstrate in the course of this *appeal*, to the satisfaction of the most incredulous mind—and may God Almighty who is the father of our Lord Jesus Christ, open your hearts to understand and believe the truth.

The *causes*, my brethren, which produce our wretchedness and miseries, are so very numerous and aggravating, that I believe the pen only of a Josephus or a Plutarch, can well enumerate and explain them. Upon subjects, then, of such incomprehensible magnitude, so impenetrable, and so notorious, I shall be obliged to omit a large class of, and content myself with giving you an exposition of a few of those, which do indeed rage to such an alarming pitch, that they cannot but be a perpetual source of terror and dismay to every reflecting mind.

I am fully aware, in making this appeal to my much afflicted and suffering brethren, that I shall not only be assailed by those whose greatest earthly desires are, to keep us in abject ignorance and wretchedness, and who are of the firm conviction that heaven has designed us and our children to be slaves and *beasts of burden* to them and their children.—I say, I do not only expect to be held up to the public as an ignorant, impudent and restless disturber of the public peace, by such avaricious creatures, as well as a mover of insubordination—and perhaps put in prison or to death, for giving a superficial exposition of our miseries, and exposing tyrants. But I am persuaded, that many of my brethren, particularly those who are ignorantly in league with slave-holders or tyrants, who acquire their daily bread by the blood and sweat of their more ignorant brethren—and not a few of those too, who are too ignorant to see an inch beyond their noses, will rise up and call me cursed—Yea, the jealous ones among us will perhaps use more abject subtlety by affirming that this work is not worth perusing; that we are well situated and there is no use in trying to better our condition, for we cannot. I will ask one question here.—Can our condition be any worse ?— Can it be more mean and abject ? If there are any changes, will they not be for the better, though they may appear for the worse at first ? Can they get us any lower ? Where can they get us ? They are afraid to treat us worse, for they know well, the day they do it they are gone. But against all accusations which may or can be preferred against me, I appeal to heaven for my motive in writing—who knows that my object is, if possible, to awaken in the breasts of my afflicted, degraded and slumbering brethren, a spirit of enquiry and investigation respecting our miseries and wretchedness in this *Republican Land of Liberty ! ! ! ! !*

The sources from which our miseries are derived and on which I shall comment, I shall not combine in one, but shall put them under distinct heads and expose them in their turn ; in doing which, keeping truth on my side, and not departing from the strictest rules of morality, I shall endeavor to penetrate, search out, and lay them open for your inspection. If you cannot or will not profit by them, I shall have done *my* duty to you, my country and my God.

And as the inhuman system of *slavery,* is the *source* from which most of our miseries proceed, I shall begin with that *curse to nations ;* which has spread terror and devastation through so many nations of antiquity, and which is raging to such a pitch at the present day in Spain and in Portugal. It had one tug in England, in France, and in the United States of America ; yet the inhabitants thereof, do not learn wisdom, and erase it entirely from their dwellings and from all with whom they have to do. The fact is, the labor of slaves comes so cheap to the avaricious usurpers, and is (as they think) of such great utility to the country where it exists, that those who are actuated by sordid avarice only, overlook the evils, which will as sure as the Lord lives, follow after the good. In fact, they are so happy to keep in ignorance and degradation, and to receive the homage and the labor of the slaves, they forget that God rules in the armies of heaven and among the inhabitants of the earth, having his ears continually open to the cries, tears and groans of his oppressed people ; and being a just and holy Being will at one day appear fully in behalf of the oppressed, and arrest the progress of the avaricious oppressors ; for although the destruction of the oppressors God may not effect by the oppressed, yet the Lord our God will bring other destructions upon them—for not

unfrequently will he cause them to rise up one
against another, to be split and divided, and to oppress each other, and sometimes to open hostilities
with sword in hand. Some may ask, what is the
matter with this enlightened and happy people ?—
Some say it is the cause of political usurpers, tyrants, oppressors, &c. But has not the Lord an
oppressed and suffering people among them ? Does
the Lord condescend to hear their cries and see
their tears in consequence of oppression ? Will he
let the oppressors rest comfortably and happy always ? Will he not cause the very children of the
oppressors to rise up against them, and oftimes put
them to death ? "God works in many ways his
" wonders to perform."

I will not here speak of the destructions which
the Lord brought upon Egypt, in consequence of
the oppression and consequent groans of the oppressed—of the hundreds and thousands of Egyptians
whom God hurled into the Red Sea for afflicting
his people in their land—of the Lor'ds suffering
people in Sparta or Lacedemon, the land of the truly
famous Lycurgus —nor have I time to comment upon
the cause which produced the fierceness with which
Sylla usurped the title, and absolutely acted as
dictator of the Roman people—the conspiracy of
Cataline—the conspiracy against, and murder of
Cæsar in the Senate house---the spirit with which
Marc Antony made himself master of the common-
wealth---his associating Octavius and Lipidus with
himself in power,---their dividing the provinces of
Rome among themselves---their attack and defeat
on the plains of Phillipi the last defenders of their
liberty, (Brutus and Cassius)---the tyranny of Tibe-
rius, and from him to the final overthrow of Con-
stantinople by the Turkish Sultan, Mahomed II.,
A. D. 1453. I say, I shall not take up time to
speak of the *causes* which produced so much wretchedness and massacre among those heathen nations,
for I am aware that you know too well, that God is

just, as well as merciful !---I shall call your attention a few moments to that *christian* nation, the
Spaniards, while I shall leave almost unnoticed that
avaricious and cruel people, the Portuguese, among
whom all true hearted christians and lovers of Jesus
Christ,. must evidently see the judgments of God
displayed. To show the judgments of God upon
the Spaniards I shall occupy but little time, leaving
a plenty of room for the candid and unprejudiced to
reflect.

All persons who are acquainted with history, and
particularly the Bible, who are not blinded by the
God of this world, and are not actuated solely by
avarice---who are able to lay aside prejudice long
enough to view candidly and impartially, things as
they were, are, and probably will be, who are willing to admit that God made man to serve him *alone*,
and that man should have no other Lord or Lords
but himself---that God Almighty is the *sole propri-
etor* or *master* of the WHOLE human family, and
will not on any consideration admit of a colleague,
being unwilling to divide his glory with another.---
And who can dispense with prejudice long enough
to admit that we are men, notwithstanding our *im-
prominent noses* and *woolly heads*, and believe that
we feel for our fathers, mothers, wives and children
as well as they do for theirs.---I say, all who are
permitted to see and believe these things, can easily
recognize the judgments of God among the Spaniards. Though others may lay the cause of the
fierceness with which they cut each other's throats,
to some other circumstances, yet they who believe
that God is a God of justice, will believe that SLA-
VERY *is the principal cause.*

While the Spaniards are running about upon the
field of battle cutting each other's throats, has not
the Lord an afflicted and suffering people in the
midst of them whose cries and groans in consequence
of oppression are continually pouring into the ears
of the God of justice ? Would they not cease to cut

each others throats if they could ? But how can
they ?   The very support which they draw from
government to aid them in perpetrating such enorm-
ities, does it not arise in a great degree from the
wretched victims of oppression among them ?   And
yet they are calling for *Peace!—Peace!!*   Will
any peace be given unto them ?   Their destruction
may indeed be procrastinated awhile, but can it
continue long while they are oppressing the Lord's
people ?   Has He not the hearts of all men in His
hand ?   Will he suffer one part of his creatures to
go on oppressing another like brutes always, with
impunity ?   And yet those avaricious wretches are
calling for *Peace ! ! ! !* I declare it does appear to
me, as though some nations think God is asleep, or
that he made the Africans for nothing else but to
dig their mines and work their farms, or they cannot
believe history, sacred or profane. I ask every man
who has a heart and is blessed with the privilege of
believing---Is not God a God of justice to all his
creatures? Do you say he is? Then if he gives peace
and tranquility to tyrants, and permits them to keep
our fathers, our mothers, ourselves and our children
in eternal ignorance and wretchedness to support
them and their families, would he be to us a God
of *justice ?*   I ask O ye *christians ! ! !* who hold us
and our children, in the most abject ignorance and
degradation, that ever a people were afflicted with
since the world began---I say, if God gives you
peace and tranquility, and suffers you thus to go on
afflicting us and our children, who have never giv-
en you the least provocation,---Would he be to us
a God of justice ?   If you will allow that we are
MEN, who feel for each other, does not the blood of
our fathers and of us their children, cry aloud to the
Lord of Sabaoth against you, for the cruelties and
murders with which you have, and do continue to
afflict us.   But it is time for me to close my remarks on the suburbs, just to enter more fully into
the interior of this system of cruelty and oppression.

ARTICLE I.

OUR WRETCHEDNESS IN CONSEQUENCE OF SLA-VERY.

My beloved brethren : The Indians of North and of South America—the Greeks—the Irish subjected under the king of Great Britain—the Jews that ancient people of the Lord—the inhabitants of the islands of the sea—in fine, all the inhabitants of the earth, (except however, the sons of Africa) are called *men*, and of course are, and ought to be free. But we, (coloured people) and our children are *brutes !!* and of course are and ought to be SLAVES to the American people and their children forever ! to dig their mines and work their farms ; and thus go on enriching them, from one generation to another with our blood and our tears !!

I promised in a preceding page to demonstrate to the satisfaction of the most incredulous, that we, (colored people of these United States of America) are the *most wretched, degraded* and abject set of beings that ever *lived* since the world began, and that the white Americans having reduced us to the wretched state of *slavery*, treat us in that condition *more cruel* (they being an enlightened and christian people) than any heathen nation did any people whom it had reduced to our condition. These affirmations are so well confirmed in the minds of all unprejudiced men who have taken the trouble to read histories, that they need no elucidation from me. But to put them beyond all doubt, I refer you in the first place to the children of Jacob, or of Israel in Egypt, under Pharaoh and his people. Some of my brethren do not know who Pharaoh and the Egyptians were—I know it to be a fact that some of them take the Egyptians to have been a gang of *devils*, not knowing any better, and that they (Egyptians) having got possession of the Lord's people, treated them *nearly* as cruel as *christians*

3

Americans do us, at the present day. For the information of such, I would only mention that the Egyptians, were Africans or colored people, such as we are—some of them yellow and others dark— a mixture of Ethiopians and the natives of Egypt— about the same as you see the colored people of the United States at the present day,—I say, I call your attention then, to the children of Jacob, while I point out particularly to you his son Joseph among the rest, in Egypt.

" And Pharaoh, said unto Joseph, thou shalt be " over my house, and according unto thy word " shall all my people be ruled; only in the throne " will I be greater than thou."*

"And Pharaoh said unto Joseph, see, I have set " thee over all the land of Egypt."†

" And Pharaoh said unto Joseph, I am Pharaoh, " and without thee shall no man lift up his hand or " foot in all the land of Egypt."‡

Now I appeal to heaven and to earth, and particularly to the American people themselves who cease not to declare that our condition is not *hard*, and that we are comparatively satisfied to rest in wretchedness and misery, under them and their children. Not, indeed, to show me a colored President, a Governor, a Legislator, a Senator, a Mayor, or an Attorney at the Bar.—But to show me a man of color, who holds the low office of a Constable, or one who sits in a Juror Box, even on a case of one of his wretched brethren, throughout this great Republic ! !—But let us pass Joseph the son of Israel a little further in review, as he existed with that heathen nation.

" And Pharaoh called Joseph's name Zaphnath- " paaneah ; and he gave him to wife Asenath the " daughter of Potipherah priest of On. And Joseph " went out over all the land of Egypt."§

Compare the above, with the American institutions. Do they not institute laws to prohibit us from

* See Genesis, chap. xli. v. 40,   †v. 41, ‡v. 44. §v. 45

marrying among the whites? I would wish, candidly, however, before the Lord, to be understood,
that I would not give a *pinch of snuff* to be married to any white person I ever saw in all the days
of my life. And I do say it, that the black man, or
man of color, who will leave his own color (provided he can get one who is good for any thing) and
marry a white woman, to be a double slave to her
just because she is *white,* ought to be treated by her
as he surely will be, viz; as a NIGER !!! It is not
indeed what I care about intermarriages with the
whites, which induced me to pass this subject in review ; for the Lord knows, that there is a day coming when they will be glad enough to get into the
company of the blacks, notwithstanding, we are, in
this generation, levelled by them almost on a level
with the brute creation ; and some of us they treat
even worse than they do the brutes that perish. I
only made this extract to show how much lower we
are held, and how much more cruel we are treated
by the Americans, than were the children of Jacob,
by the Egyptians. We will notice the sufferings of Israel some further, under *heathen Pharaoh,* compared
with ours under the *enlightened christians of America.*

" And Pharaoh spake unto Joseph, saying, thy
"father and thy brethren are come unto thee :"

" The land of Egypt is before thee : in the best
" of the land make thy father and brethren to dwell ;
" in the land of Goshen let them dwell ; and if thou
" knowest any men of activity among them, then
" make them rulers over my cattle."*

I ask those people who treat us so *well,* Oh! I
ask them, where is the most barren spot of land
which they have given unto us ? Israel had the
most fertile land in all Egypt. Need I mention the
very notorious fact, that I have known a poor man
of color, who labored night and day, to acquire a
little money, and having acquired it, he vested it in
a small piece of land, and got him a house erected

---

*Genesis, chap. xlvii. v. 5, 6.

thereon, and having paid for the whole, he moved
his family into it, where he was suffered to remain
but nine months, when he was cheated out of his
property by a white man, and driven out of door!—
And is not this the case generally? Can a man of
color buy a piece of land and keep it peaceably?
Will not some white man try to get it from him even
if it is in a *mud hole?* I need not comment any
farther on a subject, which all, both black and
white, will readily admit. But I must, really, observe that in this very city, when a man of color
dies, if he owned any real estate it must generally
fall into the hands of some white person. The wife
and children of the deceased may weep and lament
if they please, but the estate will be kept snug
enough by its white posessors.

But to prove farther that the condition of the Israelites was better under the Egyptians than ours is
under the whites. I call upon the professing christians, I call upon the philanthropist, I call upon the
very tyrant himself, to show me a page of history,
either sacred or profane, on which a verse can be
found, which maintains, that the Egyptians heaped
the *insupportable insult* upon the children of Israel
by telling them that they were not of the *human
family.* Can the whites deny this charge? Have
they not, after having reduced us to the deplorable
condition of slaves under their feet, held us up as
descending originally from the tribes of *Monkeys* or
Orang-Outangs? O! my God! I appeal to every
man of feeling—is not this insupportable? Is it not
heaping the most gross insult upon our miseries, because they have got us under their feet and we cannot
help ourselves? Oh! pity us we pray thee, Lord
Jesus, Master.—Has Mr. Jefferson declared to the
world, that we are inferior to the whites, both in the
endowments of our bodies and of minds? It is indeed surprising, that a man of such great learning,
combined with such excellent natural parts, should
speak so of a set of men in chains. I do not know

what to compare it to, unless, like putting one wild
deer in an iron cage, where it will be secured, and
hold another by the side of the same, then let it go,
and expect the one in the cage to run as fast as the
one at liberty. So far, my brethren, were the
Egyptians from heaping these insults upon their
slaves, that Pharaoh's daughter took Moses, a son
of Israel, for her own, as will appear by the following.

"And Pharaoh's daughter said unto her, [Moses'
"mother] take this child away, and nurse it for me
"and I will pay thee thy wages. And the woman
"took the child [Moses] and nursed it.

"And the child grew, and she brought him unto
"Pharaoh's daughter and he became her son. And
"she called his name Moses: and she said because
"I drew him out of the water."*

In all probability, Moses would have become
Prince Regent to the throne, and no doubt, in pro-
cess of time but he would have been seated on the
throne of Egypt. But he had rather suffer shame,
with the people of God, than to enjoy pleasures with
that wicked people for a season. O! that the colored people were long since of Moses' excellent
disposition, instead of courting favor with, and telling news and lies to our *natural enemies*, against
each other—aiding them to keep their hellish chains
of slavery upon us. Would we not long before this
time, have been respectable men, instead of such
wretched victims of oppression as we are? Would
they be able to drag our mothers, our fathers, our
wives, our children and ourselves, around the world
in chains and hand-cuffs as they do, to dig up gold
and silver for them and theirs? This question, my
brethren, I leave for you to digest; and may God
Almighty force it home to your hearts. Remember
that unless you are united, keeping your tongues
within your teeth, you will be afraid to trust your
secrets to each other, and thus perpetuate our mis-

*See Exodus, chap. ii. v. 9, 10.

eries under the *christians! ! ! ! !* [☞ADDITION,—
Remember, also to lay humble at the feet of our
Lord and Master Jesus Christ, with prayers and
fastings. Let our enemies go on with their butch-
eries, and at once fill up their cup. Never make an
attempt to gain our freedom or *natural right*, from
under our cruel oppressors and murderers, until you
see your way clear; when that hour arrives and you
move, be not afraid or dismayed ; for be you assur-
ed that Jesus Christ the king of heaven and of earth
who is the God of justice and of armies, will surely
go before you. And those enemies who have for
hundreds of years stolen our *rights*, and kept us
ignorant of Him and His divine worship, he will
remove. Millions of whom, are this day, so ignorant and avaricious, that they cannot conceive how
God can have an attribute of justice, and show mercy to us because it pleased Him to make us black—
which color, Mr. Jefferson calls unfortunate ! ! ! ! !
As though we are not as thankful to our God for having made us as it pleased himself, as they (the whites)
are for having made them white. They think because they hold us in their infernal chains of slavery
that we wish to be white, or of their color—but
they are dreadfully deceived—we wish to be just as
it pleased our Creator to have made us, and no avaricious and unmerciful wretches, have any business
to make slaves of or hold us in slavery. How would
they like for us to make slaves of, or hold them
in cruel slavery, and murder them as they do us ?
But is Mr. Jefferson's assertion true ? viz. " that
it is unfortunate for us that our Creator has been
pleased to make us black." We will not take his
say so, for the fact. The world will have an opportunity to see whether it is unfortunate for us, that
our Creator *has made us* darker than the *whites*.

Fear not the number and education of our *enemies*, against whom we shall have to contend for
our lawful right; guaranteed to us by our Maker ;
for why should we be afraid, when God is, and will

continue (if we continue humble) to be on our side?

The man who would not fight under our Lord and Master Jesus Christ, in the glorious and heavenly cause of freedom and of God—to be delivered from the most wretched, abject and servile slavery, that ever a people was afflicted with since the foundation of the world, to the present day—ought to be kept with all of his children or family, in slavery, or in chains, to be butchered by his *cruel enemies.*⌐I]

I saw a paragraph, a few years since, in a South Carolina paper, which, speaking of the barbarity of the Turks it said : " The Turks are the most bar- " barous people in the world—they treat the Greeks " more like *brutes* than human beings." And in the same paper was an advertisement, which said : " Eight well built Virginia and Maryland *Negro* "*fellows* and four *wenches* will positively be *sold* "this day *to the highest bidder !*" And what astonished me still more was, to see in this same *humane* paper!! the cuts of three men, with clubs and budgets on their backs, and an advertisement offering a considerable sum of money for their apprehension and delivery. I declare it is really so *funny* to hear the Southerners and Westerners of this country talk about *barbarity,* that it is positively, enough to make a man *smile.*

The sufferings of the Helots among the Spartans, were somewhat severe, it is true, but to say that theirs were as severe as ours among the Americans I do most strenuously deny—for instance, can any man show me an article on a page of ancient history which specifies, that, the Spartans chained, and hand-cuffed the Helots, and dragged them from their wives and children, children from their parents, mothers from their sucking babes, wives from their husbands, driving them from one end of the country to the other ? Notice the Spartans were heathens, who lived long before our Divine Master made his appearance in the flesh. Can Christian Americans

deny these barbarous cruelties? Have you not
Americans, having subjected us under you, added
to these miseries, by insulting us in telling us to
our face, because we are helpless that we are not of
the human family? I ask you, O! Americans, I
ask you, in the name of the Lord, can you deny
these charges? Some perhaps may deny, by saying, that they never thought or said that we were
not men. But do not actions speak louder than
words? –have they not made provisions for the
Greeks, and Irish? Nations who have never done
the least thing for them, while *we* who have enriched
their country with our blood and tears—have dug
up gold and silver for them and their children, from
generation to generation, and are in more miseries
than any other people under heaven, are not seen,
but by comparatively a handful of the American people? There are indeed, more ways to kill a dog
besides choaking it to death with butter. Further.
The Spartans or Lacedemonians, had some frivolous pretext for enslaving the Helots, for they (Helots) while being free inhabitants of Sparta, stirred
up an intestine commotion, and were by the Spartans subdued, and made prisoners of war. Consequently they and their children were condemned to
perpetual slavery.*

I have been for years troubling the pages of historians to find out what our fathers have done to
the *white Christians of America,* to merit such con-
dign punishment as they have inflicted on them, and
do continue to inflict on us their children. But I
must aver, that my researches have hitherto been
to no effect. I have therefore come to the im-
movable conclusion, that they (Americans) have,
and do continue to punish us for nothing else,
but for enriching them and their country. For I
cannot conceive of any thing else. Nor will I ever
believe otherwise until the Lord shall convince me,

* See Dr. Goldsmith's History of Greece—page 9. See also
Plutarch's lives. The Helots subdued by Agis, king of Sparta.

The world knows, that slavery as it existed among
the Romans, (which was the primary cause of their
destruction) was, comparatively speaking, no more
than a *cypher*, when compared with ours under the
Americans. Indeed, I should not have noticed the
Roman slaves, had not the very learned and penetrating Mr. Jefferson said, "When a master was
" murdered, all his slaves in the same house or
" within hearing, were condemned to death."*—
Here let me ask Mr. Jefferson, (but he is gone to
answer at the bar of God, for the deeds done in his
body while living,) I therefore ask the whole American people, had I not rather die, or be put to death
than to be a slave to any tyrant, who takes not only
my own, but my wife and children's lives by the
inches ? Yea, would I meet death with avidity far !
far !! in preference to such *servile submission* to the
murderous hands of tyrants. Mr. Jefferson's very
severe remarks on us have been so extensively argu-
ed upon by men whose attainments in literature, I
shall never be able to reach, that I would not have
meddled with it, were it not to solicit each of my
brethren, who has the spirit of a man, to buy a copy
of Mr. Jefferson's " Notes on Virginia," and put it
in the hand of his son. For let no one of us suppose that the refutations which have been written by
our white friends are enough—they are *whites*- —we
are *blacks*. We, and the world wish to see the
charges of Mr. Jefferson refuted by the blacks
themselves, according to their chance : for we must
remember that what the whites have written respecting this subject, is other men's labors and did not
emanate from the blacks. I know well, that there
are some talents and learning among the coloured
people of this country, which we have not a chance
to develope, in consequence of oppression ; but our
oppression ought not to hinder us from acquiring all
we can.—For we will have a chance to develope
them by and by. God will not suffer us, always to

See his notes on Virginia, page 210. 4

be oppressed. Our sufferings will come to an *end*, in spite of all the Americans this side of *eternity*. Then we will want all the learning and talents among ourselves, and perhaps more, to govern ourselves.—"Every dog must have its day," the American's is coming to an end.

But let us review Mr. Jefferson's remarks respecting us some further. Comparing our miserable fathers, with the learned philosophers of Greece, he says: "Yet notwithstanding these and other dis-"couraging circumstances among the Romans, "their slaves were often their rarest artists. They "excelled too in science, insomuch as to be usual-"ly employed as tutors to their master's children; "Epictetus, Terence and Phædrus, were slaves,— "but they were of the race of whites. It is not "their *condition* then, but *nature*, which has produced the distinction."* See this, my brethren!! Do you believe that this assertion is swallowed by millions of the whites? Do you know that Mr. Jefferson was one of as great characters as ever lived among the whites? See his writings for the world, and public labors for the United States of America. Do you believe that the assertions of such a man, will pass away into oblivion unobserved by this people and the world? If you do you are much mistaken—See how the American people treat us— have we souls in our bodies? are we men who have any spirits at all? I know that there are many *swell-bellied* fellows among us whose greatest object is to fill their stomachs. Such I do not mean—I am after those who know and feel, that we are MEN as well as other people; to them, I say, that unless we try to refute Mr. Jefferson's arguments respecting us, we will only establish them.

But the slaves among the Romans. Every body who has read history, knows, that as soon as a slave among the Romans obtained his freedom, he could rise to the greatest eminence in the State, and there

*See his notes on Virginia, page 211.

was no law instituted to hinder a slave from buying
his freedom.   Have not the Americans instituted
laws to hinder us from obtaining our freedom.   Do
any deny this charge ?   Read the laws of Virginia,
North Carolina, &c.   Further : have not the Americans instituted laws to prohibit a man of colour
from obtaining and holding any office whatever, under the government of the United States of America ?   Now, Mr. Jefferson tells us that our condition is not so hard, as the slaves were under the
Romans ! ! ! !

It is time for me to bring this article to a close.
But before I close it, I must observe to my brethren
that at the close of the first Revolution in this
country with Great Britain, there were but thirteen
States in the Union, now there are twenty-four,
most of which are slave-holding States, and the
whites are dragging us around in chains and hand-
cuffs to their new States and Territories to work
their mines and farms, to enrich them and their
children, and millions of them believing firmly that
we being a little darker than they, were made by
our creator to be an inheritance to them and their
children forever—the same as a parcel of *brutes ! !*

Are we MEN ! !—I ask you, O my brethren ! are
we MEN ? Did our creator make us to be slaves
to dust and ashes like ourselves ? Are they not dy-
ing worms as well as we ? Have they not to make
their appearance before the tribunal of heaven, to
answer for the deeds done in the body, as well as
we ? Have we any other master but Jesus Christ
alone ? Is he not their master as well as ours ?—
What right then, have we to obey and call any other master, but Himself ? How we could be so *submissive* to a gang of men, whom we cannot tell
whether they are as *good* as ourselves or not, I never could conceive.   However, this is shut up with
the Lord and we cannot precisely tell—but I declare, we judge men by their works.

The whites have always been an unjust, jealous

unmerciful, avaricious and blood thirsty set of beings, always seeking after power and authority.—
We view them all over the confederacy of Greece,
where they were first known to be any thing, (in
consequence of education) we see them there, cutting each other's throats—trying to subject each
other to wretchedness and misery, to effect which
they used all kinds of deceitful, unfair and unmerciful means. We view them next in Rome, where
the spirit of tyranny and deceit raged still higher.—
We view them in Gaul, Spain and in Britain—
in fine, we view them all over Europe, together
with what were scattered about in Asia and Africa,
as heathens, and we see them acting more like
devils than accountable men. But some may ask,
did not the blacks of Africa, and the mulattoes of
Asia, go on in the same way as did the whites of
Europe. I answer no—they never were half so avaricious, deceitful and unmerciful as the whites, according to their knowledge.

But we will leave the whites or Europeans as
heathens and take a view of them as christians, in
which capacity we see them as cruel, if not more
so than ever. In fact, take them as a body, they are
ten times more cruel avaricious and unmerciful than
ever they were; for while they were heathens they
were bad enough it is true, but it is positively a fact
that there were not quite so audacious as to go and
take vessel loads of men, women and children, and
in cold blood and through devilishness, throw them
into the sea, and murder them in all kind of ways.
While they were heathens, they were too ignorant for such barbarity. But being christians,
enlightened and sensible, they are completely prepared for such hellish cruelties. Now suppose God
were to give them more sense, what would they do.
If it were possible would they not *dethrone* Jehovah and seat themselves upon his throne ? I therefore, in the name and fear of the Lord God of heav-
en and of earth, divested of prejudice either on the

side of my colour or that of the whites, advance my suspicion of them, whether they are *as good by nature* as we are or not. Their actions, since they were known as a people, have been the reverse, I do indeed suspect them, but this, as I before observed, is shut up with the Lord, we cannot exactly tell, it will be proved in succeeding generations.— The whites have had the essence of the gospel as it was preached by my master and his apostles—the Ethiopians have not, who are to have it in its meridian splendor—the Lord will give it to them to their satisfaction. I hope and pray my God, that they will make good use of it, that it may be well with them.

ARTICLE II.

OUR WRETCHEDNESS IN CONSEQUENCE OF IGNORANCE.

Ignorance, my brethren, is a mist, low down into the very dark and almost impenetrable abyss of which, our fathers for many centuries have been plunged. The christians, and enlightened of Europe, and some of Asia, seeing the ignorance and consequent degradation of our fathers, instead of trying to enlighten them, by teaching them that religion and light with which God had blessed them, they have plunged them into wretchedness ten thousand times more intolerable, than if they had left them entirely to the Lord, and to add to their miseries, deep down into which they have plunged them, tell them, that they are an *inferior* and *distinct race* of beings, which they will be glad enough to recall and swallow by and by. Fortune and misfortune, two inseparable companions, lay rolled up in the wheel of events, which have from the creation of the world, and will continue to take place among men until God shall dash worlds together.

When we take a retrospective view of the arts

and sciences—the wise legislators—The Pyramids,
and other magnificent buildings—the turning of the
channel of the river Nile, by the sons of Africa or
of Ham, among whom learning originated, and was
carried thence into Greece, where it was improved
upon and refined. Thence among the Romans,
and all over the then enlightened parts of the world,
and it has been enlightening the dark and benighted
minds of men from then, down to this day. I say,
when I view retrospectively, the renown of that
once mighty people, the children of our great pro-
genitor, I am indeed cheered. Yea further, when I
view that mighty son of Africa, HANNIBAL, one of
the greatest generals of antiquity, who defeated and
cut off so many thousands of the white Romans or
murderers, and who carried his victorious arms, to
the very gate of Rome, and I give it as my candid
opinion, that had Carthage been well united and
had given him good support, he would have carried
that cruel and barbarous city by storm. But they
were disunited, as the colored people are now, in
the United States of America, the reason our natural enemies are enabled to keep their feet on our
throats.

Beloved brethren—here let me tell you, and believe it, that the Lord our God, as true as he sits
on his throne in heaven, and as true as our Saviour
died to redeem the world, will give you a Hannibal,
and when the Lord shall have raised him up, and
given him to you for your possession, O my suffering brethren ! remember the d ivisions and consequent sufferings of *Carthage* and of *Hayti*. Read
the history particularly of Hayti, and see how they
were butchered by the whites, and do you take
warning. The person whom God shall give you,
give him your support and let him go his length, and
behold in him the salvation of your God. God will
indeed, deliver you through him from your deplorable and wretched condition under the christians of
America. I charge you this day before my God to
lay no obstacle in his way, but let him go.

The whites want slaves, and want us for their slaves, but some of them will curse the day they ever saw us. As true as the sun ever shone in its meridian splendor, my colour will root some of them out of the very face of the earth. They shall have enough of making slaves of, and butchering, and murdering us in the manner which they have. No doubt some may say that I write with a bad spirit, and that I being a black, wish these things to occur. Whether I write with a bad or a good spirit, I say if these things do not occur in their proper time, it is because the world in which we live does not exist, and we are deceived with regard to its existence. It is immaterial however to me, who believe, or who refuse—though I should like to see the whites repent peradventure God may have mercy on them, some however, have gone so far that their cup must be filled.

But what need have I to refer to antiquity, when Hayti, the glory of the blacks and terror of tyrants, is enough to convince the most avaricious and stupid of wretches—which is at this time, and I am sorry to say it, plagued with that scourge of nations, the Catholic religion; but I hope and pray God that she may yet rid herself of it, and adopt in its stead the Protestant faith; also, I hope that she may keep peace within her borders and be united, keeping a strict look [out for tyrants, for if they get the least chance to injure her, they will avail themselves of it, as true as the Lord lives in heaven. But one thing which gives me joy is, that they are men who would be cut off to a man, before they would yield to the combined forces of the whole world—in fact, if the whole world was combined against them, it could not do any thing with them, unless the Lord delivers them up.

Ignorance and treachery one against the other— a servile and abject submission to the lash of tyrants, we see plainly, my brethren, are not the natural elements of the blacks, as the Americans try to make us believe ; but these are misfortunes which God has suffered our fathers to be enveloped in for many ages, no doubt in consequence of their disobedience to their Maker, and which do, indeed, reign at this time among us, almost to the destruction of all other principles : for I must truly say, that ignorance, the mother of treachery and deceit, gnaws into our very vitals. Ignorance, as it now exists among us, pro-. duces a state of things, Oh my Lord ! too horrible to present to the world. Any man who is curious to see the full force of ignorance developed among the colored people of the United States of America, has only to go into the southern and western states of this confederacy, where, if he is not a tyrant, but has the feelings of a human being, who can feel for a fellow creature, he may see enough to make his very heart bleed ! He may see there, a son take his mother, who bore almost the pains of death to give him birth, and by the command of a tyrant, strip her as naked as she came into the world, and apply the cow-hide to her, until she falls a victim to death in the road ! He may see a husband take his dear wife, not unfrequently in a pregnant state, and perhaps far advanced, and beat her for an unmerciful wretch, until his infant falls a lifeless lump at her feet ! Can the Americans escape God Almighty ? If they do, can he be to us a God of Justice ? God is just, and I know it—for he has convinced me to my satisfaction—I cannot doubt him. My observer may see fathers beating their sons, mothers their daughters, and children their parents, all to pacify the passions of unrelenting tyrants. He may also, see them telling news and lies, making mischief one upon another. These are some of the productions of ignorance, which he will see practised among my dear brethren, who are held in unjust slavery and wretchedness, by avaricious and unfeeling tyrants, to whom, and their hellish deeds, I would suffer my life to be taken before I would submit. And when my curious observer comes to take notice of those who are said to be free (which assertion I deny) and who are making some frivolous pretensions to common sense, he will see that branch of ignorance among the slaves assuming a more cunning and deceitful course of procedure. He may see some of my brethren in league with tyrants, selling their own brethren into *hell upon earth*, not dissimilar to the exhibitions in Africa but in a more secret, servile and abject manner. Oh Heaven! I am full!!! I can hardly move my pen !!! As I expect some one will try to put me to death, to strike terror into others, and to obliterate from their minds the notion of freedom, so as to keep my brethren the more secured in wretchedness where they will be permitted to stay but a short time (whether tyrants believe it or not,) I shall give the world a development of facts which are already witnessed in the courts of heaven. My observer may see some of those ignorant and treacherous creatures (colored people) sneaking about in the large cities, endeavoring to find out all strange colored people, where they work and where they reside, asking them questions and trying to ascertain whether they are runaways or not, telling them, at the same time, that they always have been, are, and always will be, friends to their brethren; and perhaps, that they themselves are absconders, and a thousand such treacherous lies to get the better information of the more ignorant!! There have been and are at this day in Boston, New York, Philadelphia, and Baltimore, coloured men, who are in league with tyrants, and receive a great portion of their daily bread, of the moneys which they acquire from the blood and tears of their more miserable brethren whom they scandalously delivered into the hands of our *natural enemies ! ! ! !*

To show the force of degraded ignorance and deceit among us some further, I will give here an extract from a paragraph, which may be found in the Columbian Centinel of this city, for September 9,

1829, on the first page of which the curious may
find an article, headed

" AFFRAY AND MURDER."

" *Portsmouth, (Ohio) Aug.* 22, 1829.

" A most shocking outrage was committed in
" Kentucky, about eight miles from this place, on
" the 14th inst. A negro driver, by the name of
" Gordon, who had purchased in Maryland about
" sixty negroes, was taking them, assisted by an
" associate named Allen and the wagoner who con-
" veyed the baggage, to the Mississippi. The men
" were hand-cuffed and chained together, in the
" usual manner for driving these poor wretches.
" while the women and children were suffered to
" proceed without incumbrance. It appears that,
" by means of a file the negroes unobserved had suc-
" ceeded in separating the irons which bound their
" hands, in such a way as to be able to throw them
" off at any moment. About 8 o'clock in the morn-
" ing, while proceeding on the state road leading
" from Greenup to Vanceburg, two of them dropped
" their shackles and commenced a fight, when the
" wagoner (Petit) rushed in with his whip to com-
" pel them to desist. At this moment, every negro
" was found to be perfectly at liberty; and one of
" them seizing a club, gave Petit a violent blow on
" the head and laid him dead at his feet ; and Allen,
" who came to his assistance, met a similar fate
" from the contents of a pistol fired by another of
" the gang. Gordon was then attacked, seized and
" held by one of the negroes, whilst another fired
" twice at him with a pistol, the ball of which each
" time grazed his head, but not proving effectual,
" he was beaten with clubs, and left for dead They
" then commenced pillaging the wagon and with an
" axe split open the trunk of Gordon and rifled it
" of the money, about $2,490.   Sixteen of the ne-
" groes then took to the woods ; Gordon, in the
" mean time, not being materially injured was

" enabled, by the assistance of one of the women,
" to mount his horse and flee ; pursued, however,
" by one of the gang on another horse, with a drawn
" pistol ; fortunately he escaped with his life, barely
" arriving at a plantation, as the negro came in
" sight ; who then turned about and retreated.

" The neighborhood was immediately rallied,
" and a hot pursuit given—which, we understand,
" has resulted in the capture of the whole gang and
" the recovery of the greatest part of the money.—
" Seven of the negro men and one woman, it is said
" were engaged in the murder, and will be brought
" to trial at the next court in Greenupsburg."

Here my brethren, I want you to notice particularly in the above article, the ignorant and *deceitful
actions* of this colored woman. I beg you to view
it carefully, as for ETERNITY ! ! ! Here a *notorious
wretch*, with two other confederates had SIXTY of
them in a gang, driving them like *brutes*—the men
all in chains and hand-cuffs, and by the help of God
they got their chains and hand-cuffs thrown off and
caught two of the wretches and put them to death,
and beat the other until they thought he was dead,
and left him for dead ; however he deceived them,
and rising from the ground, this *servile woman*
helped him upon his horse and he made his escape.
Brethren what do you think of this ? Was it the
natural *fine feelings* of this woman, to save such a
wretch alive ? I know that the blacks, take them
half enlightened and ignorant, are more humane and
merciful than the most enlightened and refined Europeans that can be found in all the earth. Let no
one say that I assert this because I am prejudiced
on the side of my color, and against the whites or
Europeans. For what I write, I do it candidly,
for my God and the good of both parties : Natural
observations have taught me these things ; there is
a solemn awe in the hearts of the blacks, as it res-
pects *murdering* men :* whereas the whites (though
they are great cowards) where they have the advan-

—* Which is the reason the whites take the advantage of us.

tage, or think that there are any prospects of getting it, they murder all before them, in order to subject men to wretchedness and degradation under them. This is the natural result of pride and avarice.—But I declare, the actions of this black woman are really insupportable. For my own part, I cannot think it was any thing but servile deceit, combined with the most gross ignorance : for we must remember that *humanity, kindness* and the *fear of the Lord*, does not consist in protecting *devils.* Here is a set of wretches, who had SIXTY of them in a gang, driving them around the country like *brutes*, to dig up gold and silver for them, (which they will get enough of yet.) Should the lives of such creatures be spared ? Is GOD and Mammon in league ? What has the Lord to do with a gang of desperate wretches, who go *sneaking about the country like robbers*—light upon his people wherever they can get a chance, binding them with chains and hand-cuffs, beat and murder them as they would *rattle-snakes?* Are they not the Lord's enemies? Ought they not to be destroyed ? Any person who will save such wretches from destruction, is fighting against the Lord, and will receive his just recompense. The black men acted like *blockheads.* Why did they not make sure of the wretch ? He would have made sure of them if he could. It is just the way with black men—eight white men can frighten fifty of them ; whereas, if you can only get courage into the blacks, I do declare it, that one good black man can put to death six white men ; and I give it as a fact, let twelve black men get well armed for battle, and they will kill and put to flight fifty whites. The reason is, the blacks, once you get them started, they glory in death. The whites have had us under them for more than three centuries, murdering, and treating us like brutes ; and, as Mr. Jefferson wisely said, they have never *found us out*—they do not know, indeed, that there is an unconquerable dis-position in the breasts of the blacks, which when it

is fully awakened and put in motion, will be subdued, only with the destruction of the animal existence. Get the blacks started, and if you do not
have a gang of lions and tigers to deal with, I am a
deceiver of the blacks and the whites. How sixty
of them could let that wretch escape unkilled, I cannot conceive—they will have to suffer as much for
the two whom they secured, as if they had put one
hundred to death : if you commence, make sure
work—do not trifle, for they will not trifle with you
—they want us for their slaves, and think nothing
of murdering us in order to subject us to that wretched condition—therefore, if there is an *attempt* made
by us, kill or be killed. Now, I ask you had you
not rather be killed than to be a slave to a tyrant,
who takes the life of your mother, wife, and dear little
children? Look upon your mother, wife and children,
and answer God Almighty ; and believe this, that
it is no more harm for you to kill a man, who is trying to kill you, than it is for you to take a drink of
water when thirsty ; in fact, the man who will stand
still and let another murder him, is worse than an
infidel, and if he has common sense, ought not to
to be pitied.—The actions of this deceitful and
ignorant coloured woman, in saving the life of a
desperate man, whose avaricious and cruel object
was to drive her and her companions in miseries,
through the country like cattle, to make his fortune
on their carcasses, are but too much like that of
thousands of our brethren in these states : if any
thing is whispered by one, which has any allusion
to the melioration of their dreadful condition, they
run and tell tyrants, that they may be enabled to
keep them the longer in wretchedness and miseries.
Oh ! coloured people of these United States, I
ask you, in the name of that God who made us,
have we, in consequence of oppression, nearly lost
the spirit of man, and, in no very trifling degree,
adopted that of brutes ? Do you answer, No ?—
I ask you, then, what set of men can you point me

to, in all the world, who are so abjectly employed
by their oppressors as we are by our *natural enemies?* How can, Oh! how can those enemies but
say that we and our children are not of the HUMAN
FAMILY, but were made by our creator to be an inheritance to them and theirs forever? How can the
slave-holders but say that they can bribe the best
coloured person in the country, to sell his brethren
for a trifling sum of money, and take that atrocity
to confirm them in their avaricious opinion, that we
were made to be slaves to them and their children?
How could Mr. Jefferson but say, *" I advance it
" therefore as a suspicion only, that the blacks,
" whether originally a distinct race, or made dis-
" tinct by time and circumstances, are *inferior* to
" the whites in the endowments both of body and
" mind?" " It," says he, "is not against experience
" to suppose, that different species of the same
" genus, or varieties of the same species, may pos-
" sess different qualifications." [Here, my brethren
listen to him.] ☞ " Will not a lover of natural
" history then, one who views the gradations in all
" the races of *animals* with the eye of philosophy,
" excuse an effort to keep those in the department
" of MAN as *distinct* as nature has formed them?"
I hope you will try to find out the meaning of this
verse—its widest sense and all its bearings: whether you do or not, remember the whites do. This
very verse, brethren, having emanated from Mr.
Jefferson, a much greater philosopher the world
never afforded, has in truth injured us more, and has
been as great a barrier to our emancipation as any
thing that has ever been advanced against us. I
hope you will not let it pass unnoticed. He goes on
further, and says: " This *unfortunate* difference of
" colour, and *perhaps* of *faculty*, is a powerful ob-
" stacle to the emancipation of these people. Many
" of their advocates, while they wish to vindicate the

---

*See his Notes on Virginia, page 213.

" liberty of human nature are anxious also to pre-
" serve its *dignity* and *beauty*. Some of these, em-
" barrassed by the question, ' What further is to be
" done with them? join themselves in opposition
" with those who are actuated by sordid avarice
" only." Now I ask you candidly, my suffering
brethren in time, who are candidates for the eternal
worlds, how could Mr. Jefferson but have given the
world these remarks respecting us, when we are so
submissive to them, and so much servile deceit pre-
vails among ourselves—when we so *meanly* submit
to their murderous lashes, to which neither the Indians or any other people under heaven would submit? No, they could die to a man, before they
would suffer such things from men who are no better than themselves, and *perhaps not so good*. Yes,
how can our friends but be embarrassed, as Mr.
Jefferson says, by the question, " What further is
to be done with these people?" for while they are
working for our emancipation, we are, by our
treachery, wickedness and deceit, working against
ourselves and our children—helping ours, and the
enemies of God, to keep us and our dear little children, in their infernal chains of slavery ! ! Indeed,
our friends cannot but relapse and join themselves
with those who are [actuated by *sordid avarice*
only ! ! ! ! ' For my part, I am glad Mr. Jefferson has advanced his position for your sake ; for
you will either have to contradict or confirm him
by your own actions and not by what our friends
have said or done for us; for those things are other
men's labors and do not satisfy the Americans who
are waiting for us to prove to them ourselves that
we are MEN before they will be willing to admit the
fact ; for I pledge you my sacred word of honor
that Mr. Jefferson's remarks respecting us have sunk
deep into the hearts of millions of the whites and
never will be removed this side of eternity. For
how can they, when we are confirming him every
day by our *groveling submissions* and *treachery ?*

I aver that when I look upon these United States and see the ignorant deceptions and consequent wretchedness of my brethren, I am brought oft-times solemnly to a stand, and in the midst of my reflections I exclaim to my God, 'Lord didst thou make us to be slaves to our brethren, the whites ?' But when I reflect that God is just, and that millions of my wretched brethren would meet death with glory—yea, more, would plunge into the very mouths of cannons and be torn into particles as minute as the atoms which compose the elements of the earth, in preference to a mean submission to the lash of tyrants, I am with streaming eyes, compelled to shrink back into nothingness before my Maker, and exclaim again, thy will be done, O Lord God Almighty.

Men of colour, who are also of sense, for you particularly is my appeal designed. Our more ignorant brethren are not able to penetrate its value. I call upon you therefore to cast your eyes upon the wretchedness of your brethren and to do your utmost to enlighten them—*go to work and enlighten your brethren !*—let the Lord see you doing what you can to rescue them and yourselves from degradation. Do any of you say that you and your family are free and happy and what have you to do with wretched slaves and other people ? So can I say, for I enjoy as much freedom as any of you, if I am not quite as well off as the best of you. Look into our freedom and happiness and see of what kind they are composed !! They are of the very lowest kind—they are the very *dregs !*—they are the most servile and abject kind, that ever a people was in possession of! If any of you wish to know how FREE you are, let one of you start and go thro' the southern and western States of this country, and unless you travel as a slave to a white man (a servant is a *slave* to the man whom he serves,) or have your free papers (which if you are not careful they will get from you) if they do not take you up and put you in jail, and if you cannot give evidence of your freedom, sell you into eternal slavery, I am not a living man; or any man of color, immaterial who he is or where he came from, if he is not the 4th from the "*Negro race*," (as we are called,) the white christians of America will serve him the same, they will sink him into wretchedness & degradation forever while he lives. And yet some of you have the hardihood to say that you are free & happy! May God have mercy on your freedom and happiness! I met a colored man in the street a short time since, with a string of boots on his shoulder; we fell into conversation, and in course of which I said to him, what a miserable set of people we are! He asked why?— Said I, we are so subjected under the whites, that we cannot obtain the comforts of life, but by cleaning their boots and shoes, old clothes, waiting on them, shaving them, etc. Said he, (with the boots on his shoulders,) " I am completely happy !!! I never want to live any better or happier than when I can get a plenty of boots and shoes to clean !!!" Oh ! how can those who are actuated by avarice only, but think that our creator made us to be an inheritance to them forever, when they see that our greatest glory is centered in such mean and low objects ? Understand me, brethren, I do not mean to speak against the occupations by which we acquire enough and sometimes scarcely that, to render ourselves and families comfortable through life. I am subjected to the same inconvenience, as you all. My objections are, to our *glorying* and being *happy* in such low employments; for if we are men, we ought to be thankful to the Lord for the past, and for the future. Be looking forward with thankful hearts to higher attainments than *wielding the razor* and *cleaning boots and shoes.* The man whose aspirations are not *above*, and even *below* these, is indeed, ignorant and wretched enough. I advance it therefore to you, not as a *problematical*, but as an unshaken and forever immoveable *fact*, that your full glory and happiness, as well as all other colored people un-

6

der heaven, shall never be fully consummated, but
with the *entire emancipation of your enslaved brethren all over the world.* You may therefore, go to
work and do what you can to rescue, or join in
with tyrants to oppress them and yourselves, until
the Lord shall come upon you all like a thief in the
night. For I believe it is the will of the Lord
that our greatest happiness shall consist in working
for the salvation of our whole body. When this is
accomplished a burst of glory will shine upon you,
which will indeed astonish you and the world. Do
any of you say this will never be done? I assure
you that God will accomplish it—if nothing else
will answer, he will hurl tyrants and devils into
atoms and make way for his people. But O my
brethren! I say unto you again, you must go to
work and *prepare the way* of the Lord.

There is a great work for you to do, as trifling
as some of you may think of it. You have to prove
to the Americans and the world, that we are MEN,
and not *brutes* as we have been represented, and by
millions treated. Remember, to let the aim of your
labours among your brethren, and particularly the
youths, be the dissemination of education and religion. It is lamentable, that many of our children
go to school, from four until they are eight or ten,
and sometimes fifteen years of age, and leave school
knowing but a little more about the grammar of their
language than a horse does about handling a mus-
ket—and not a few of them are really so ignorant,
that they are unable to answer a person correctly,
general questions in geography, and to hear them
read would only be to disgust a man who has a
taste for reading; which, to do well, as trifling as
it may appear to some, (to the ignorant in particu-
lar) is a great part of learning. Some few of them,
may make out to scribble tolerably well, over a half
sheet of paper, which I believe has hitherto been a
powerful obstacle in our way, to keep us from ac-
cquiring knowledge. An ignorant father, who knows

no more than what nature has taught him, together with what little he acquires by the senses of hearing and seeing, finding his son able to write a neat hand, sets it down for granted that he has as good learning as any body ; the young, ignorant gump, hearing his father or mother, who perhaps may be ten times more ignorant, in point of literature, than himself, extolling his learning, struts about in the full assurance, that his attainments in literature are sufficient to take him through the world, when, in fact, he has scarcely any learning at all ! ! ! !

I promiscuously fell in a conversation once, with an elderly colored man on the topics of education, and of the great prevalency of ignorance among us: Said he, " I know that our people are very ignorant " but my son has a good education : he can write as " well as any white man, and I assure you that no " one can fool him," etc. Said I, what else can your son do, besides writing a good hand ? Can he post a set of books in a mercantile manner ? Can he write a neat piece of composition in prose or in verse ? To these interrogations he answered in the negative. Said I, Did your son learn, while he was at school, the width and depth of English Grammar? to which he also replied in the negative, telling me his son did not learn those things. Your son, said I, then, has hardly any learning at all—he is almost as ignorant, and more so, than many of those who never went to school one day in their lives. My friend got a little put out, and so walking off said that his son could write as well as any white man.— Most of the coloured people, when they speak of the education of one among us who can write a neat hand, and who perhaps knows nothing but to scribble and puff pretty fair on a small scrap of paper, immaterial whether his words are grammatical, or spelt correctly, or not; if it only looks beautiful, they say he has as good an education as any white man—he can write as well as any white man, etc.

The poor, ignorant creature, hearing this, he is ashamed, forever after, to let any person see him humbling himself to another for knowledge but going about trying to deceive those who are more ignorant than himself, he at last falls an ignorant victim to death in wretchedness. I pray that the Lord may undeceive my ignorant brethren, and permit them to throw away pretensions, and seek after the substance of learning. I would crawl on my hands and knees through mud and mire, to the feet of a learned man, where I would sit and humbly supplicate him to instil into me, that which neither devils nor tyrants could remove, only with my life—for the Africans to acquire learning in this country, makes tyrants quake and tremble on their sandy foundation. Why what is the matter? Why, they know that their infernal deeds of cruelty will be made known to the world. Do you suppose one man of good sense and learning would submit himself, his father, mother, wife and children, to be slaves to a wretched man like himself, who, instead of compensating him for his labours, chains, handcuffs and beats him and family almost to death, leaving life enough in them, however, to work for, and call him master? No! no! he would cut his devilish throat from ear to ear, and well do slaveholders know it. The bare name of educating the coloured people, scares our cruel oppressors almost to death. But if they do not have enough to be frightened for yet, it will be, because they can always keep us ignorant, and because God approbates their cruelties, with which they have been for centuries murdering us. The whites shall have enough of the blacks, yet, as true as God sits on his throne in heaven.

Some of our brethren are so very full of learning that you cannot mention any thing to them which they do not know better than yourself!!—nothing is strange to them!!—they knew every thing years ago! —if any thing should be mentioned in company where they are, immaterial how important it is respecting us or the world, if they had not divulged it; they make light of it, and affect to have known it long before it was mentioned, and try to make all in the room, or wherever you may be, believe that your conversation is nothing—not worth hearing !! All this is the result of ignorance and ill-breeding ; for a man of good breeding, sense, and penetration, if he had heard a subject told twenty times over and should happen to be in company where one should commence telling it again, he would wait with patience on its narrator, and see if he would tell it as it was told in his presence before—paying the most strict attention to what is said, to see if any more light will be thrown on the subject ; for all men are not gifted alike in telling, or even hearing the most simple narration. These ignorant, vicious, and wretched men, contribute almost as much injury to our body as tyrants themselves, by doing so much for the promotion of ignorance amongst us ; for they, making such pretensions to knowledge, such of our youth as are seeking after knowledge, and can get access to them, take them as criterions to go by, who will lead them into a channel, where, unless the Lord blesses them with the privilege of seeing their error, they will be irretrievably lost forever, while in time !!

I must close this article by narrating the very heart-rending fact, that I have examined school-boys and young men of colour in different parts of the country, in the most simple parts of Murray's English Grammar, and not more than one in thirty was able to give a correct answer to my interrogations. If any one contradicts me, let him step out of his door into the streets of Boston, New York, Philadelphia. or Baltimore, (no use to mention any other, for the Christians are too charitable further south or west !) —I say, let him who disputes me, step out of his door into the streets of either of those four cities,

and promiscuously collect one hundred school boys
or young men of colour, *who have been to school,*
and who are considered by the coloured people to
have received an excellent education, because, perhaps, some of them can write a good hand, but who
notwithstanding their neat writing, may be almost
as ignorant, in comparison, as horses.　And, I say
it, he will hardly find (in this enlightened day, and
in the midst of this *charitable* people) five in one
hundred, who are able to correct the false grammar
of their language.　The cause of this almost
universal ignorance amongst us, I appeal to
our school-masters to declare.　Here is a fact,
which I this very minute take from the mouth of a
young coloured man, who has been to school in this
state (Massachusetts) nearly nine years, and who
knows grammar this day, *nearly* as well as he did
the day he first entered the school-house, under a
white master.　This young man says—" My mas-
" ter would never allow me to study grammar."—
I asked him why ?　" The school committee," said
he, " forbid the colored children learning grammar
" —they would not allow any but the white child-
" ren to study grammar."　It is a notorious fact that
the major part of the white Americans have, ever
since we have been among them, tried to keep us
ignorant and make us believe that God made us and
our children to be slaves to them and theirs.　*Oh !*
my God, have mercy on Christian Americans ! !

ARTICLE III.

OUR WRETCHEDNESS IN CONSEQUENCE OF THE
PREACHERS OF THE RELIGION OF JESUS CHRIST.

RELIGION, my brethren, is a substance of deep
consideration among all nations of the earth.　The
Pagans have a kind, as well as the Mahometans,
the Jews and the Christians.　But pure and unde-

filed religion, such as was preached by Jesus Christ
and his apostles, is hard to be found in all the earth.
God, through his instrument, Moses, handed a dispensation of his divine will to the children of Israel
after they had left Egypt for the land of Canaan, or
of Promise, who through hypocrisy, oppression, and
unbelief, departed from the faith. He then, by his
apostles handed a dispensation of his, together with
the will of Jesus Christ, to the Europeans in Europe, who, in open violation of which, have made
merchandize of us, and it does appear as though
they take this very dispensation to aid them in their
infernal depredations upon us. Indeed, the way in
which religion was and is conducted by the Europeans and their descendants, one might believe it
was a plan fabricated by themselves and the *devils*
to oppress us. But hark! my master has taught
me better than to believe it—he has taught me that
his gospel as it was preached by himself and his
apostles remains the same, notwithstanding Europe
has tried to mingle blood and oppression with it.

It is well known to the Christian world that Bar-
tholomew Las Casas, that very notoriously avaricious Catholic priest or preacher, and adventurer
with Columbus in his second voyage, proposed to
his countrymen, the Spaniards in Hispaniola, to import the Africans from the Portuguese settlement in
Africa, to dig up gold and silver, and work their
plantations for them, to effect which, he made a
voyage thence to Spain, and opened the subject to
his master, Ferdinand, then in declining health, who
listened to the plan ; but who died soon after, and
left it in the hands of his successor, Charles V.*—
This wretch, (" Las Cassas, the Preacher,") suc-
ceeded so well in his plans of oppression, that in
1503, the first blacks had been imported into the
new world. Elated with this success, and stimulated
by sordid avarice only, he importuned Charles V. in

* See Butler's History of the United States, vol. 1, page 24.
See also, page 25.

1511, to grant permission to a Flemish merchant to import 4000 blacks at one time. Thus we see, through the instrumentality of a pretended preacher of the gospel of Jesus Christ our common master, our wretchedness first commenced in America— where it has been continued from 1503 to this day, 1829. A period of three hundred and twenty-six years. But two hundred and nine, from 1620— when twenty of our fathers were brought into James-town, Virginia, by a Dutch man-of-war, and sold off like brutes to the highest bidders ; and there is not a doubt in my mind, but that tyrants are in hopes to perpetuate our miseries under them and their children until the final consummation of all things. But if they do not get dreadfully. deceived, it will be because God has forgotten them.

The Pagans, Jews and Mahometans try to make proselytes to their religions, and whatever human beings adopt their religions, they extend to them their protection. But Christian Americans not on-ly hinder their fellow creatures, the Africans, but thousands of them will *absolutely beat a coloured person nearly to death, if they catch him on his knees, supplicating the throne of grace.* This barba-rous cruelty was by all the heathen nations of anti-quity, and is by the Pagans, Jews and Mahometans of the present day, left entirely to Christian Ameri-cans to inflict on the Africans and their descendants that their cup which is nearly full may be completed. I have known tyrants or usurpers of human liberty in different parts of this country take their fellow crea-tures, the colored people, and beat them until they would scarcely leave life in them ; what for ? Why they say, " The black devils had the audacity to be " found *making prayers and supplications to the* " *God who made them ! ! !*" Yes, I have known small collections of coloured people to have con-vened together, for no other purpose than to wor-ship God Almighty, in spirit and in truth, to the best of their knowledge ; when tyrants, calling themselves *patrols*, would also convene and wait almost in breathless silence for the poor coloured people to commence singing and praying to the Lord our God, and as soon as they had commenced the wretches would burst in upon them and drag them out and commence beating them as they would rattle-snakes—many of whom, they would beat so unmercifully, that they would hardly be able to crawl for weeks and sometimes for months.—Yet the American ministers send out missionaries to convert the heathen, while they keep us and our children sunk at their feet in the most abject ignorance and wretchedness that ever a people was afflicted with since the world began. Will the Lord suffer this people to proceed much longer? Will he not stop them in their career? Does he regard the heathens abroad, more than the heathens among the Americans? Surely the Americans must believe that God is partial, notwithstanding his Apostle Peter, declared before Cornelius and others that he has no respect to persons, but in every nation he that feareth God and worketh righteousness is accepted with him.—"The word," said he, "which God " sent unto the children of Israel, preaching peace, " by Jesus Christ, (he is the Lord of all.")* Have not the Americans the Bible in their hands? Do they believe it? Surely they do not. See how they treat us in open violation of the Bible!! They no doubt will be greatly offended with me, but if God does not awaken them, it will be, because they are superior to other men, as they have represented themselves to be. Our divine Lord and Master said "all things whatsoever ye would that men should " do unto you, do ye even so unto them." But an American minister, with the Bible in his hand, holds us and our children in the most abject slavery and wretchedness. Now I ask them, would they like for us to hold them and their children in abject slavery and wretchedness? No says one, that ne-

---

*See the Acts of the Apostles, chap. x. v.—25—26.

ver can be done—you are too abject and ignorant
to do it—you are not men—you were made to be
slaves to us, to dig up gold and silver for us and
our children. Know this, my dear sirs, that although
you treat us and our children now, as you do your
domestic beasts—yet the final result of all future
events are known but to God Almighty alone, who
rules in the armies of heaven and among the inhabitants of the earth, and who dethrones one earthly
king and sits up another, as it seemeth good in his
holy sight. We may attribute these vicissitudes to
what we please, but the God of armies and of justice rules in heaven and in earth, and the whole
American people shall see and know it yet, to their
satisfaction. I have known pretended preachers of
the gospel of my Master, who not only held us as
their natural inheritance, but treated us with as
much rigor as any Infidel or Deist in the world—
just as though they were intent only on taking our
blood and groans to glorify the Lord Jesus Christ.
The wicked and ungodly, seeing their preachers
treat us with so much cruelty, they say : our preachers, who must be right, if any body are, treat them
like brutes, and why cannot we ?—They think it is
no harm to keep them in slavery and put the whip to
them, and why cannot we do the same!—They being preachers of the gospel of Jesus Christ, if it
were any harm, they would surely preach against
their oppression and do their utmost to erase it from
the country ; not only in one or two cities, but one
continual cry would be raised in all parts of this
confederacy, and would cease only with the complete overthrow of the system of slavery, in every
part of the country. But how far the American
preachers are from preaching against slavery and
oppression, which have carried their country to the
brink of a precipice ; to save them from plunging
down the side of which, will hardly be effected, will
appear in the sequel of this paragraph, which I
shall narrate just as it transpired. I remember a
Camp Meeting in South Carolina, for which I em-

barked in a Steam Boat at Charleston, and having
been five or six hours on the water, we at last arriv-
ed at the place of hearing, where was a very great
concourse of people, who were no doubt, collected
together to hear the word of God, (that some had
collected barely as spectators to the scene, I will
not here pretend to doubt, however, that is left to
themselves and their God.) Myself and boat companions, having been there a little while, we were
all called up to hear; I among the rest, went up
and took my seat—being seated, I fixed myself in a
complete position to hear the word of my Saviour
and to receive such as I thought was authenticated
by the Holy Scriptures; but to my no ordinary as-
tonishment, our Reverend gentleman got up and
told us (colored people) that slaves must be obedient to their masters—must do their duty to their
masters or be whipped—the whip was made for the
backs of fools, &c. Here I pause for a moment, to
give the world time to consider what was my sur-
prise, to hear such preaching from a minister of my
Master, whose very gospel is that of peace and not
of blood and whips, as this pretended preacher tried
to make us believe. What the American preachers
can think of us, I aver this day before my God, I
have never been able to define. They have news-
papers and monthly periodicals, which they receive
in continual succession, but on the pages of which,
you will scarcely ever find a paragraph respecting
slavery, which is ten thousand times more injurious
to this country than all the other evils put together;
aud which will be the final overthrow of its government, unless something is very speedily done; for
their cup is nearly full.—Perhaps they will laugh at,
or make light of this; but I tell you Americans!
that unless you speedily alter your course, *you* and
your *Country are gone ! ! ! ! ! !* For God Almighty
will tear up the very face of the earth ! ! ! ! Will not
that very remarkable passage of Scripture be fulfilled
on Christian Americans? Hear it Americans ! !
" He that is unjust, let him be unjust still :—and he

" which is filthy, let him be filthy still : and he that
" is righteous, let him be righteous still ; and he
" that is holy, let him be holy still."* I hope that
the Americans may hear, but I am afraid that they
have done us so much injury, and are so firm in the
belief that our Creator made us to be an inheritance
to them forever, that their hearts will be hardened,
so that their destruction may be sure.—This language, perhaps is too harsh for the American's delicate ears. But Oh Americans! Americans!! I
warn you in the name of the Lord, (whether you
will hear, or forbear,) to repent and reform, or you
are ruined!!!!!! Do you think that our blood is hid-
den from the Lord, because you can hide it from the
rest of the world by sending out missionaries, and
by your charitable deeds to the Greeks, Irish, &c. ?
Will he not publish your secret crimes on the house
top ? Even here in Boston, pride and prejudice have
got to such a pitch, that in the very houses erected
to the Lord, they have built little places for the reception of colored people, where they must sit during meeting, or keep away from the house of God ;
and the preachers say nothing about it---much less,
go into the hedges and highways seeking the lost
sheep of the house of Israel, and try to bring them
in, to their Lord and Master. There are hardly a
more wretched, ignorant, miserable, and abject set
of beings in all the world, than the blacks in the
Southern and Western sections of this country, under tyrants and devils. The preachers of America
cannot see them, but they can send out missionaries
to convert the heathens, notwitnstanding. Americans ! unless you speedily alter your course of proceeding, if God Almighty does not stop you, I say it
in his name, that you may go on and do us you
please for ever, both in time and eternity—never
fear any evil at all ! ! ! ! ! ! ! !

[☞ADDITION.—The preachers and people of the
the United States form societies against Free Ma-

---

* See Revelation, chap. xxii. v. 11.

sonry and Intemperance, and write against Sabbath breaking, Sabbath mails, Infidelity, &c. &c. But the fountain head,* compared with which all those other evils are comparatively nothing, and from the bloody and murderous head of which, they receive no trifling support, is hardly noticed by the Americans. This is a fair illustration of the state of society in this country—it shows what a bearing *avarice* has upon a people, when they are nearly given up by the Lord to a hard heart and a reprobate mind, in consequence of afflicting their fellow creatures. God suffers some to go on until they are ruined for ever !! Will it be the case with our brethren the whites of the United States of America ? We hope not—we would not wish to see them destroyed, notwithstanding they have and do now treat us more cruel than any people have treated another, on this earth since it came from the hands of its creator (with the exception of the French and the Dutch, they treat us nearly as bad as the Americans of the United States.) The will of God must however, in spite of us, *be done.*

The English are the best friends the colored people have upon earth. Tho' they have oppressed us a little, and have colonies now in the West Indies, which oppress us *sorely,*—Yet notwithstanding they (the English) have done one hundred times more for the melioration of our condition, than all the other nations of the earth put together. The blacks cannot but respect the English as a nation, notwithstanding they have treated us a little cruel.

There is no intelligent *black man* who knows any thing, but esteems a real English man, let him see him in what part of the world he will—for they are the greatest benefactors we have upon earth. We have here and there, in other nations, good friends. But as a nation, the English are our friends.⌐]

How can the preachers and people of America believe the Bible ? Does it teach them any distinction on account of a man's color ? Hearken, Amer-

---

* Slavery and oppression.

icans! to the injunctions of our Lord and Master, to
his humble followers.

* " And Jesus came and spake unto them saying,
" all power is given unto me in heaven and in earth.

" Go ye, therefore, and teach all nations, baptiz-
" ing them in the name of the Father, and of the
" Son, and of the Holy Ghost,

" Teaching them to observe all things whatsoever
" I have commanded you ; and lo, I am with you
" alway, even unto the end of the world.   Amen."

I declare, that the very face of these injunctions
appears to be of God and not of man. They do not
show the slightest degree of distinction.   " Go ye,
" therefore," (says my divine Master) and teach all
" nations," (or in other words, all people) " baptiz-
" ing them in the name of the Father, and of the
" Son, and of the Holy Ghost."   Do you understand the above, Americans ?   We are a people,
notwithstanding many of you doubt it.   You have
the Bible in your hands, with this very injunction.
Have you been to Africa, teaching the inhabitants
thereof the words of the Lord Jesus ?   " Baptizing
" them in the name of the Father, and of the Son,
" and of the Holy Ghost."   Have you not, on the
contrary, entered among us, and learnt us the art of
throat-cutting, by setting us to fight, one against
another, to take each other as prisoners of war, and
sell to you for small bits of calicoes, old swords,
knives, &c. to make slaves for you and your children ?   This being done, have you not brought us
among you, in chains and handcuffs, like brutes,
and treated us with all the cruelties and rigour
your ingenuity could invent, consistent with the laws
of your country, which (for the blacks) are tyrannical enough ?   Can the American preachers appeal
unto God, the Maker and Searcher of hearts, and
tell him, with the Bible in their hands, that they
make no distinction on account of men's colour ?

---

* See St. Matthew's Gospel, chap. xxviii. v. 18—19—20. After
Jesus was risen from the dead.

Can they say, O God! thou knowest all things—
thou knowest that we make no distinction between
thy creatures to whom we have to preach thy Word?
Let them answer the Lord ; and if they cannot do
it in the affirmative, have they not departed from
the Lord Jesus Christ, their master ? But some
may say, that they never had or were in possession
of a religion, which makes no distinction, and of
course they could not have departed from it. I ask
you then, in the name of the Lord, of what kind can
your religion be ? Can it be that which was preached by our Lord Jesus Christ from Heaven ? I believe you cannot be so wicked as to tell him that
his Gospel was that of *distinction*. What can the
American preachers and people take God to be ?—
Do they believe his words ? If they do, do they
believe that he will be mocked? Or do they believe
because they are whites and we blacks, that God
will have respect to them ? Did not God make us
as it seemed best to himself ? What right, then,
has one of us, to despise another and to treat him
cruel, on account of his colour, which none but the
God who made it can alter ? Can there be a greater absurdity in nature, and particularly in a free republican country ? But the Americans, having in-
troduced slavery among them, their hearts have become almost seared, as with an hot iron, and God
has nearly given them up to believe a lie in preference to the truth ! ! ! and I am awfully afraid that
pride, prejudice, avarice and blood, will, before
long, prove the final ruin of this happy republic, or
land of liberty ! ! ! Can any thing be a greater
mockery of religion than the way in which it is conducted by the Americans? It appears as though
they are bent only on daring God Almighty to do
his best—they chain and handcuff us and our children and drive us around the country like brutes,
and go into the house of the God of justice to return Him thanks for having aided him in their infernal cruelties inflicted upon us. Will the Lord
suffer this people to go on much longer, taking his

holy name in vain ? Will he not stop them, PREACH-
ERS and all ? O Americans ! Americans ! ! I call
God—I call angels—I call men, to witness, that
your DESTRUCTION *is at hand*, and will be speedily
consummated unless you REPENT.

ARTICLE IV.

OUR WRETCHEDNESS IN CONSEQUENCE OF THE COLONIZING PLAN.

My dearly beloved brethren :—This is a scheme
on which so many able writers, together with that
very judicious colored Baltimorean, have comment-
ed, that I feel my delicacy about touching it.   But
as I am compelled to do the will of my master, I declare, I will give you my sentiments upon it.   Pre-
vious, however, to giving my sentiments, either for
or against it, I shall give that of Mr. Henry Clay,
together with that of Mr. Elias B. Caldwell, Esq. of
the District of Columbia, as extracted from the National Intelligencer, by Dr. Torrey, author of a series of " Essays on Morals, and the Diffusion of Use-
ful Knowledge."

At a meeting which was convened in the District
of Columbia, for the express purpose of agitating
the subject of colonizing us in some part of the
world, Mr. Clay was called to the chair, and having
been seated a little while, he rose and spake, in
substance, as follows : Says he—*" That class of
" the mixt population of our country [coloured peo-
" ple] was peculiarly situated; they neither enjoyed
" the immunities of freemen, nor were they subject-
" ed to the incapacities of slaves, but partook, in
" some degree, of the qualities of both.   From their
" condition, and the unconquerable prejudices re-
" sulting from their colour, they never could amal-
" gamate with the free whites of this country.   It

* See Dr. Torrey's Portraiture of Domestic Slavery in the
United States, page 85—86.

" was desirable, therefore, as it respected them, and
" the residue of the population of the country, to
" drain them off. Various schemes of colonization
" had been thought of, and a part of our continent,
" it was supposed by some, might furnish a suita-
" ble establishment for them. But, for his part,
" Mr. C. said, he had a decided preference for some
" part of the coast of Africa. There ample provision
" might be made for the colony itself, and it might
" be rendered instrumental in the introduction into
" that extensive quarter of the globe, of the arts,
" civilization, and Christianity." [Here I ask Mr.
Clay, what kind of Christianity? Did he mean
such as they have among the Americans—distinction, whip, blood and oppression? I pray the Lord
Jesus Christ to forbid it.] "There," said he,
" was a peculiar, a moral fitness, in restoring them
" to the land of their fathers, and if instead of
" the evils and sufferings which we had been the in-
" nocent cause of inflicting upon the inhabitants of
" Africa, we can transmit to her the blessings of
" our arts, our civilization, and our religion. May
" we not hope that America will extinguish a great
" portion of that moral debt which she has contract-
" ed to that unfortunate continent? Can there be
" a nobler cause than that which, whilst it proposes,
&c. * * * * * * [you know what this means.]
" contemplates the spreading of the arts of civilized
" life, and the possible redemption from ignorance
" and barbarism of a benighted quarter of the globe?"
    Before I proceed any further, I solicit your no-
tice, brethren, to the foregoing part of Mr. Clay's
speech, in which he says, (☞ look above) "and
" if, instead of the evils and sufferings, which we
" had been the innocent cause of inflicting," &c.
What this very learned statesman could have been
thinking about, when he said in his speech, "we had
" been the innocent cause of inflicting," etc., I
have never been able to conceive. Are Mr. Clay
and the rest of the Americans, innocent of the blood
8

and groans of our fathers and us, their children?
Every individual may plead innocence, if he pleases,
but God will, before long, separate the innocent
from the guilty, unless something is speedily done—
which I suppose will hardly be, so that their destruction may be sure. Oh Americans! let me tell
you, in the name of the Lord, it will be good
for you, if you listen to the voice of the Holy
Ghost, but if you do not you are ruined!!!! Some
of you are good men ; but the will of my God must
be done. Those avaricious and ungodly tyrants
among you, I am awfully afraid will drag down the
vengeance of God upon you.—When God Almighty
commences his battle on the continent of America,
for the oppression of his people, tyrants will wish
they never were born.

But to return to Mr. Clay, whence I digressed.
He says, "It was proper and necessary distinctly
" to state, that he understood it constituted no part
" of the object of this meeting, to touch or agitate
" in the slightest degree, a delicate question, con-
" nected with another portion of the coloured popu-
" lation of our country. It was not proposed to
" deliberate upon or consider at all, any question of
" emancipation, or that which was connected with
" the abolition of slavery. It was upon that condi-
" tion alone, he was sure, that many gentlemen from
" the South and the West, whom he saw present,
" had attended, or could be expected to co-operate.
" It was on that condition only, that he himself
" had attended."—That is to say, to fix a plan
to get those of the coloured people, who are said to
be free, away from among those of our brethren
whom they unjustly hold in bondage, so that they
may be enabled to keep them the more secure in
ignorance and wretchedness, to support them and
their children, and consequently they would have
the more obedient slaves. For if the free are allow-
ed to stay among the slaves, they will have inter-
course together, and, of course, the free will learn
the slaves *bad habits*, by teaching them that they

are MEN, as well as other people, and certainly
ought, and *must* be FREE.

I presume, that every intelligent man of colour
must have some idea of Mr. Henry Clay, originally of Virginia, but now of Kentucky ; they
know too, perhaps, whether he is a friend, or a
foe, to the coloured citizens of this country, and
of the world. This gentleman, according to his
own words, had been highly favoured and blessed
of the Lord, though he did not acknowledge
it ; but to the contrary, he acknowledged men, for
all the blessings which God had favoured him.
At a public dinner given him at Fowler's Garden,
Lexington, Kentucky, he delivered a public speech
to a very large concourse of people—in the concluding clause of which, he says, "And now, my
" friends and fellow citizens, 1 cannot part from
" you, on possibly the last occasion of my ever pub-
" licly addressing you, without reiterating the ex-
" pression of my thanks, from a heart overflowing
" with gratitude. I came among you, now more
" than thirty years ago, an orphan boy pennyless, a
" stranger to you all, without friends without the fa-
" vour of the great, you tookme up, cherished me,
" protected me, honoured me, you have constantly
" poured upon me a bold and unabated stream of in-
" numerable favors, time which wears out every
" thing has increased and strengthened your affec-
" tion for me. When I seemed deserted by almost
" the whole world, and assailed by almost every
" tongue, and pen, and press, you have fearlessly
" and manfully stood by me, with unsurpassed zeal
" and undiminished friendship. When I felt as if I
" should sink beneath the storm of abuse and de-
" traction, which was violently raging around me,
" I have found myself upheld and sustained by your
" encouraging voices and approving smiles. I have
" doubtless, committed many faults and indiscre-
" tions, over which you have thrown the broad man-
" tle of your charity. But I can say, and in the
" presence of God and this assembled multitude, I
" will say, that I have honestly and faithfully serv-

" ed my country—that I have never wronged it—
" and that, however unprepared, I lament that I am
" to appear in the Divine presence on other ac-
" counts, I invoke the stern justice of his judgment
" on my public conduct without the slightest ap-
" prehension of his displeasure."

Hearken to this statesman indeed, but no philanthropist, whom God sent into Kentucky, an orphan
boy, pennyless and friendless, where he not only
gave him a plenty of friends and the comforts of life,
but raised him almost to the very highest honour in
the nation, where his great talents, with which the
Lord has been pleased to bless him, has gained for
him the affection of a great portion of the people with
whom he had to do.   But what has this gentleman
done for the Lord, after having done so much for
him ?   The Lord has a suffering people, whose
moans and groans at his feet for deliverance from
oppression and wretchedness, pierce the very throne
of Heaven, and call loudly on the GOD of Justice,
to be revenged.   Now what this gentleman who is
so highly favored of the Lord, has done to liberate
those miserable victims of oppression, shall appear
before the world, by his letters to Mr. Gallatin,
Envoy Extraordinary and Minister Plenipotentiary
to Great Britain, dated June 19, 1826.   Though
Mr. Clay was writing for the states, yet nevertheless, it appears, from the very face of his letters to
that gentleman, that he was as anxious, if not more
so, to get those free people and sink them into
wretchedness, as his constituents for whom he wrote.

The Americans of North and of South America,
including the West India Islands—no trifling portion of whom were, for stealing, murdering, &c.
compelled to flee from Europe, to save their necks
or banishment, have effected their escape to this
continent, where God blessed them with all the
comforts of life—He gave them a plenty of every
thing calculated to do them good—not satisfied with
this, however, they wanted slaves, and wanted us
for their slaves, who belong to the Holy Ghost, and

no other, who we shall have to serve instead of tyrants. I say, the Americans want us, the property
of the Holy Ghost, to serve them. But there is a
day fast approaching when (unless there is a universal repentance on the part of the whites, which
will scarcely take place—they have got to be so hardened in consequence of our blood, and so wise in
their own conceit.) To be plain and candid with
you, Americans! I say that the day is fast approaching when there will be a greater time on the continent of America than ever was witnessed upon this
earth since it came from the hands of its Creator. Some
of you have done us so much injury that you will never be able to repent. Your cup must be filled. You
want us for your slaves and shall have enough of us
—God is just, *who will give you your fill of us.* But
Mr. Henry Clay, speaking to Mr. Gallatin respecting coloured people who had effected their escape
from the U. States (or to them *hell upon earth ! !*)
to the hospitable shores of Canada* from whence it
would cause more than the lives of the Americans
to get them, to plunge into wretchedness—he says:
" The General Assembly of Kentucky, one of the
states which is most affected by the escape of slaves
into Upper Canada, has again, at their session
which has just terminated, invoked the interposi-
tion of the General Government. In the treaty
which has been recently concluded with the United Mexican States, and which is now under the
consideration of the Senate, provision is made for
the restoration of fugitive slaves. As it appears
from your statements of what passed on that subject with the British Plenipotentiaries, that they
admitted the correctness of the principle of restoration, it is hoped that you will be able to succeed in
making satisfactory arrangements."
There are a series of these letters, all of which are
to the same amount ; some however presenting a
face more of his own responsibility. I wonder what
would this gentleman think if the Lord should give

* Among the English, our real friends and benefactors.

him among the rest of his blessings enough of slaves?
Could he blame any other being but himself? Do
we not belong to the Holy Ghost? What business
has he or any body else, to be sending letters about
the world respecting us? Can we not go where we
want to, as well as other people, only if we obey the
voice of the Holy Ghost? This gentleman, (Henry Clay) not only took an active part in this colonizing plan, but was absolutely chairman of a meeting
held at Washington the 21st day of December, 1816*
to agitate the subject of colonizing us in Africa.—
Now I appeal and ask every citizen of these United
States and of the world, both *white* and *black*, who has
any knowledge of Mr. Clay's public labors for these
States—I want you candidly to answer the Lord,
who sees the secrets of your hearts, Do you believe
that Mr. Henry Clay, late Secretary of State, and
now in Kentucky, is a friend to the blacks, further
than his personal interest extends? Is it not his
greatest object and glory upon earth to sink us into
miseries and wretchedness by making slaves of us,
to work his plantation to enrich him and his family?
Does he care a pinch of snuff about Africa—whether it remains a land of Pagans and of blood, or of
Christians, so long as he gets enough of her sons and
daughters to dig up gold and silver for him? If he
had no slave, and could obtain them in no other way
if it were not repugnant to the laws of his country,
which prohibit the importation of slaves, (which act
was indeed more through apprehension than humanity) would he not try to import a few from Africa to
work his farm? Would he work in the hot sun to
earn his bread if he could make an African work for
nothing, particularly if he could keep him in ignorance and make him believe that God made him for
nothing else but to work for him? Is not Mr. Clay
a white man, and too delicate to work in the hot
sun? Was he not made by his Creator to sit in the
shade, and make the blacks work without remuner-

---

* In the first edition of this work, it should read 1816, as above,
and not 1826, as it there appears.

ation for their services, to support him and his family? I have been for some time taking notice of this man's speeches and public writings, but never to my knowledge have I seen any thing in his writings which insisted on the emancipation of slavery, which has almost ruined his country. Thus we see the depravity of men's hearts, when in pursuit only of gain—particularly when they oppress their fellow creatures to obtain that gain—God suffers some to go on until they are lost for ever. This same Mr. Clay wants to know what he has done to merit the disapprobation of the American people. In a public speech delivered by him, he asked : " Did I in-" volve my country in an unnecessary war ?" to merit the censure of the Americans—" Did I bring " obloquy upon the nation, or the people whom I " represented—did I ever lose an opportunity to " advance the fame, honor and prosperity of this " State and the Union ?" How astonishing it is, for a man who knows so much about God and his ways, as Mr. Clay, to ask such frivolous questions. Does he believe that a man of his talents and standing in the midst of a people, will get along unnoticed by the penetrating and all-seeing eye of God who is continually taking cognizance of the hearts of men ? Is not God against him, for advocating the murderous cause of slavery ? If God is against him, what can the Americans, together with the whole world do for him ? Can they save him from the hand of the Lord Jesus Christ ?

I shall now pass in review the speech of Mr. Elias B. Caldwell, Esq. of the District of Columbia, extracted from the same page on which Mr. Clay's will be found. Mr. Caldwell, giving his opinion respecting us, at that ever memorable meeting, he says : " The more you improve the condition of " these people, the more you cultivate their minds, " the more miserable you make them in their pre-" sent state. You give them a higher relish for " those privileges which they can never attain, and " turn what we intend for a blessing into a curse."

Let me ask this benevolent man, what he means by
a blessing intended for us ? Did he mean sinking
us and our children into ignorance and wretchedness, to support him and his family ? What he
meant will appear evident and obvious to the most
ignorant in the world. ☞ See Mr. Caldwell's intended blessings for us, O ! my Lord ! ! ! " No,"
said he, " if they must remain in their present situa-
" tion, keep them in the *lowest state of degradation*
" *and ignorance.* The nearer you bring them to
" the condition of brutes, the better chance do you
" give them of possessing their *apathy.*" Here I
pause to get breath, having labored to extract the
above clause of this gentleman's speech, at that colonizing meeting. I presume that every body knows
the meaning of the word "*apathy*"—if they do not,
let him get Sheridan's Dictionary, where he will
find it explained in full. I solicit the attention of
the world to the foregoing part of Mr. Caldwell's
speech, that they may see what man will do with
his fellow men, when he has them under his feet.
To what length will not man go in iniquity, when
given up to a hard heart and reprobate mind, in
consequence of blood and oppression ? The last
clause of this speech, which was written in a very
artful manner and which will be taken for the speech
of a friend, without close examination and deep penetration, I shall now present. He says, " Surely
Americans ought to be the last people on earth
to advocate such slavish doctrines, to cry peace
and contentment to those who are deprived of the
privileges of civil liberty, they who have so large-
ly partaken of its blessings, who know so well
how to estimate its value, ought to be among the
foremost to extend it to others." The real sense
and meaning of the last part of Mr. Caldwell's speech
is, get the free people of colour away to Africa,
from among the slaves, where they may at once be
blessed and happy, and our slaves will be contented
to rest in ignorance and wretchedness, to dig up gold
and silver for us and our children. Men have in-

deed, got to be so cunning, these days, that it would take the eye of a Solomon to penetrate and find them out.

Extract from the speech of Mr. John Randolph, of Roanoke.

Said he :—"It had been properly observed by the " Chairman, as well as by the gentlemen from this " District (meaning Messrs. Clay and Caldwell) " that there was nothing in the proposition submit- " ted to consideration which in the smallest degree " touches another very important and delicate ques- " tion, which ought to be left as much out of view " as possible, (Negro Slavery.)*

"There was no fear, Mr. R. said, that this prop- " osition would alarm the slave-holders ; they had " been accustomed to think seriously of the sub- " ject. There was a popular work on agriculture, " by John Taylor of Carolina, which was wide- " ly circulated, and much confided in, in Virginia. " In that book, much read because coming from a " practical man, this description of people, [refer- " ring to us half free ones,] were pointed out as a " great evil. They had indeed been held up as the " greater bug-bear to every man who feels an incli- " nation to emancipate his slaves, not to create in " the bosom of his country so great a nuisance. If " a place could be provided for their reception, and " a mode of sending them hence, there were hun- " dreds, nay thousands of citizens, who would, by " manumitting their slaves, relieve themselves from " the cares attendant on their possession. The " great slave-holder, Mr. R. said, was frequently a " mere sentry at his own door—bound to stay on " his plantation to see that his slaves were properly

---

* " Niger" is a word derived from the Latin, which was used by the old Romans to designate inanimate beings which were black, such as soot, pot, wood, house, &c. Also, of animals which they considered inferior to the human species, as a black horse, cow, hog, bird, dog, &c. The white Americans have applied this term to Africans, by way of reproach for our color, to aggra. vate and heighten our miseries, because they have their feet on our throats, and we cannot help ourselves.

" treated, &c.   Mr. R. concluded by saying that
" he had thought it necessary to make these re-
" marks, being a slave-holder himself, to show that,
" so far from being connected with abolition of
" slavery, the measure proposed would prove one of
" greatest securities to enable the master to keep
" in possession his own property."

Here is a demonstrative proof, of a plan got up
by a gang of slave-holders to select the free people
of colour from among the slaves, that our more
miserable brethren may be the better secured in ignorance and wretchedness, to work their farms and
dig their mines, and thus go on enriching the christians with their blood and groans.   What our brethren could have been thinking about, who have left
their native land and home and gone away to Africa I am unable to say.   This country is as much
ours as it is the whites, whether they will admit it now
or not, they will see and believe it by and by.   They
tell us about prejudice—what have we to do with
it ?   Their prejudices will be obliged to fall like
lightning to the ground, in succeeding generations ;
not, however with the will and consent of all the
whites, for some will be obliged to hold on to the
old adage, viz. : the blacks are not men, but were
made to be an inheritance to us and our children
forever ! ! ! ! ! ! I hope the residue of the coloured
people will stand still and see the salvation of God,
and the miracle which he will work for our delivery
from wretchedness under the christians ! ! ! ! ! !

[☞ ADDITION.—If any of us see fit to go away,
go to those who have been for many years, and are
now our greatest earthly friends and benefactors—
the English. If not so, go to our brethren, the Hay-
tians, who, according to their word, is bound to
protect and comfort us.   The Americans say that
we are ungrateful—but I ask them for heaven's sake,
what we should be grateful to them for—for murdering our fathers and mothers ?—Or do they wish
us to return thanks to them for chaining and hand-
cuffing us, branding us, cramming fire down our

throats, or for keeping us in slavery, and beating us nearly or quite to death to make us work in ignorance and miseries, to support them and their families. They certainly think that we are a gang of fools. Those among them, who have volunteered their services for our redemption, though we are unable to compensate them for their labors, we nevertheless thank them from the bottom of our hearts, and have our eyes steadfastly fixed upon them, and their labors of love for God and man. But do slaveholders think that we thank them for keeping us in miseries, and taking our lives by the inches? ⌷⌷]

Before I proceed further with this scheme, I shall give an extract from the letter of th t truly Reverend Divine, (Bishop Allen,) of Philadelphia, respecting this trick. At the instance of the Editor of the Freedom's Journal, he says, * "Dear Sir, I " have been for several years trying to reconcile my " mind to the Colonizing of Africans in Liberia, " but there have always been, and there still re " main great and insurmountable objections against " the scheme. We are an unlettered people, " brought up in ignorance, not one in a hundred can " read or write, not one in a thousand has a liberal " education; is there any fitness for such to be sent " into a far country, among heathens, to convert or " civilize them, when they themselves are neither " civilized or christianized? See the great bulk of " the poor, ignorant Africans in this country, ex " posed to every temptation before them: all for " the want of their morals being refined by educa " tion and proper attendance paid unto them by " their owners, or those who had the charge of " them. It is said by the Southern slave-holders, " that the more ignorant they can bring up the Afri " cans, the better slaves they make, 'go and come.' " Is there any fitness for such people to be colonized " in a far country, to be their own rulers? Can we " not discern the project of sending the free people " of colour away from their country? Is it not for

*See Freedom's Journal for Nov. 2d, 1827—vol. 1, No. 34.

" the interest of the slave-holders to select the free
" people of colour out of the different states, and
" send them to Liberia? Will it not make their
" slaves uneasy to see free men of colour enjoying
" liberty? It is against the law, in some of the
" southern states, that a person of colour should
" receive an education, under a severe penalty. Co-
" lonizationists speak of America being first colo-
" nized, but is there any comparison between the
" two? America was colonized by as *wise, judi-*
" *cious* and *educated* men as the world afforded.
" WILLIAM PENN did not want for *learning, wis-*
,' *dom, or intelligence.* If all the people in Europe
" and America were as ignorant, and in the same
" situation as our brethren, what would become of
" the world? where would be the principle or piety
" that would govern the people? We were *stolen*
" from our mother country, and brought *here.* We
" have *tilled* the ground and made fortunes for thou-
" sands, and still they are not weary of our services.
" *But they who stay to till the ground must be*
" *slaves.* Is there not land enough in America, or
" 'corn enough in Egypt?' Why should they send
" us into a far country to die? See the thousands
" of foreigners emigrating to America every year:
" and if there be ground sufficient for them to cul-
" tivate, and bread for them to eat; why would
" they wish to send the *first tillers* of the land away?
" Africans have made fortunes for thousands, who
" are yet unwilling to part with their services; but
" the free must be sent away, and those who remain
" must be *slaves.* I have no doubt that there are
" many good men who do not see as I do, and who
" are for sending us to Liberia; but they have not
" duly considered the subject—they are not men of
" colour. This land which we have watered with
" our *tears* and *our blood,* is now our *mother country,*
" and we are well satisfied to stay where wisdom
" abounds and the gospel is free."

" RICHARD ALLEN,
" *Bishop of the African Methodist Episcopal*
" *Church in the United States.*"

I have given you, my brethren, an extract verbatim from the letter of that godly man as you may find it on the aforementioned page of Freedom's Journal. I know that thousands and perhaps millions of my brethren in these States, have never heard of such a man as Bishop Allen---a man whom God many years ago raised up among his ignorant and degraded brethren, to preach Jesus Christ and him crucified to them---who notwithstanding, had to wrestle against principalities and the powers of darkness to diffuse that gospel with which he was endowed, among his brethren—but who having overcome the combined powers of devils and wicked men has under God planted a church among us which will be as durable as the foundation of the earth on which it stands. Richard Allen! O my God!! the bare recollection of the labours of this man, and his ministers among his deplorably wretched brethren (rendered so by the whites,) to bring them to a knowledge of the God of heaven, fills my soul with all those very high emotions which would take the pen of an Addison to portray. It is impossible, my brethren, for me to say much in this work respecting that man of God. When the Lord shall raise up coloured historians in succeeding generations, to present the crimes of this nation to the then gazing world, the Holy Ghost will make them do justice to the name of Bishop Allen, of Philadelphia. Suffice it for me to say, that the name of this very man (Richard Allen,) though now in obscurity and degradation, will notwithstanding stand on the pages of history among the greatest divines who have lived since the apostolic age, and among the African's, Bishop Allen's will be entirely pre-eminent. My brethren, search after the character and exploits of this godly man among his ignorant and miserable brethren, to bring them to a knowledge of the truth as it is in our Master. Consider upon the tyrants nd false christians against whom he had to contend order to get access to his brethren. See him and

his ministers in the states of New York, New Jersey,
Penn. Delaware and Maryland, carrying the glad-
some tidings of free and full salvation to the colored people. Tyrants and false christians however,
would not allow him to penetrate far into the South
for fear that he would awaken some of his ignorant
brethren, whom they held in wretchedness and miseries—for fear, I say it, that he would awaken and
bring them to a knowledge of their Maker. O my
Master ! my Master ! I cannot but think upon
Christian Americans ! ! What kind of people can
they be ? Will not those whc were burnt up in
Sodom and Gomorrah rise up in judgment against
Christian Americans with the Bible in their hands,
and condemn them ? Will not the Scribes and
Pharisees of Jerusalem, who had nothing but the
laws of Moses and the Prophets to go by, rise up in
judgment against Christian Americans, and condemn them* who in addition to these have a revelation from Jesus Christ the son of the living God? In
fine, will not the Antediluvians, together with the
whole heathen world of antiquity, rise up in judgment against Christian Americans and condemn
them ? The Christians of Europe and America go
to Africa, bring us away, and throw us into the seas,
and in other ways murder us, as they would wild
beasts. The Antediluvians and heathens never
dreamed of such barbarities. Now the Christians
believe because they have a name to live, while they
are dead, that God will overlook such things. But
if he does not deceive them, it will be because he
has overlooked it sure enough. But to return to this
godly man, Bishop Allen. I do hereby openly affirm it to the world, that he has done more in a
spiritual sense for his ignorant and wretched brethren than any other man of colour has, since the
world began. And as for the greater part of the

---

*I mean those whose labors for the good, or rather destruction
of Jerusalem, and the Jews. Ceased before our Lord entered
the Temple, and over turned the tables of the Money Changers.

whites, it has hitherto been their greatest object and glory to keep us ignorant of our Maker, so as to make us believe that we were made to be slaves to them and their children to dig up gold and silver for them. It is notorious that not a few professing christians among the whites who profess to love our Lord and Saviour Jesus Christ, have assailed this man and laid all the obstacles in his way they possibly could, consistent with their profession—and what for ? Why, their course of proceeding and his, clashed exactly together—they trying their best to keep us ignorant that we might be the better and more obedient slaves—while he on the other hand, doing his very best to enlighten us and teach us a knowledge of the Lord. And I am sorry that I have it to say, that many of our brethren have joined in with our oppressors, whose dearest objects are only to keep us ignorant and miserable, against this man to stay his hand. However, they have kept us in so much ignorance that many of us know no better than to fight against ourselves, and by that means strengthen the hands of our natural enemies, to rivet their infernal chains of slavery upon us and our children. I have several times called the white Americans our *natural enemies*—I shall here define my meaning of the phrase. Shem, Ham, and Japheth, together with their father Noah and wives, I believe were not natural enemies to each other. When the ark rested after the flood upon Mount Arrarat in Asia, they (eight) were all the people which could be found alive in all the earth—in fact if scriptures be true (which I believe are) there were no other living men in all the earth, notwithstanding some ignorant creatures hesitate not to tell us, that we, (the blacks) are the seed of Cain, the murderer of his brother Abel. But where those ignorant and avaricious wretches could have got their information, I am unable to declare. Did they receive it from the Bible ? I have searched the Bible as well as they, if I am not as well learned as they are, and have never seen a verse which testifies

whether we are the seed of Cain or of Abel.—
Yet those men tell us that we are of the seed of Cain
and that God put a dark stain upon us, that we
might be known as their slaves!!! Now I ask
those avaricious and ignorant wretches, who act
more like the seed of Cain, by murdering, the whites
or the blacks? How many vessel loads of human
beings have the blacks thrown into the seas? How
many thousand souls have the blacks murdered in
cold blood to make them work in wretchedness and
ignorance, to support them and their families?*—
However, let us be the seed of Cain, Harry, Dick
or Tom!!! God will show the whites what we are
yet. I say, from the beginning, I do not think that
we were natural enemies to each other. But the
whites having made us so wretched, by subjecting
us to slavery, and having murdered so many millions
of us in order to make us work for them, and out of
devilishness—and they taking our wives, whom we
love as we do ourselves—our mothers who bore the
pains of death to give us birth—our fathers & dear
little children, and ourselves, and strip and beat us
one before the other—chain, handcuff and drag us
about like rattle-snakes—shoot us down like wild
bears, before each other's faces, to make us submissive to and work to support them and their families. They (the whites) know well if we are *men*—
and there is a secret monitor in their hearts which
tells them we are—they know, I say, if we *are* men,
and see them treating us in the manner they do,
that there can be nothing in our hearts but death
alone, for them; notwithstanding we may appear
cheerful, when we see them murdering our dear
mothers and wives, because we cannot help ourselves. Man, in all ages and all nations of the
earth, is the same. Man is a peculiar creature—he

---

*How many millions souls of the human family have the blacks,
beat nearly to death, to keep them from learning to read the Word
of God and from writing. And telling lies about them, by holding
them up to the world as a tribe of TALKING APES, void of
intellect!!! incapable of LEARNING, &c.

is the image of his God, though he may be subjected to the most wretched condition upon earth, yet
that spirit and feeling which constitute the creature
man, can never be entirely erased from his breast,
because the God who made him after his own image,
planted it in his heart; he cannot get rid of it. The
whites knowing this, they do not know what to do;
they are afraid that we, being men, and not brutes,
will retaliate, and woe will be to them; therefore, that dreadful fear, together with an avaricious
spirit, and the natural love in them to be called
masters, (which term we will yet honour them with
to their sorrow) bring them to the resolve that
they will keep us in ignorance and wretchedness, as
long as they possibly can* and make the best of their
time while it lasts. Consequently they, themselves,
(and not us) render themselves our natural enemies,
by treating us so cruel. They keep us miserable now,
and call us their property, but some of them will
have enough of us by and by—their stomachs shall
run over with us; they want us for their slaves, and
shall have us to their fill. (We are all in the world
together!!) I said above, because we cannot help
ourselves, (viz. we cannot help the whites murdering
our mothers and our wives) but this statement is in-
correct—for we can help ourselves; for, if we lay
aside abject servility, and be determined to act like

---

*And still hold us up with indignity as being incapable of ac-
quiring knowledge !!! See the inconsistency of the assertions of
those wretches—they beat us inhumanly, sometimes almost to
death, for attempting to inform ourselves, by reading the *Word* of
our Maker, and at the same time tell us, that we are beings *void of
intellect!!!!!* How admirably their practices agree with their pro-
fessions in this case. Let me cry shame upon you Americans, for
such outrages upon human nature!!! If it were possible for the
whites always to keep us ignorant and miserable, and make us
work to enrich them and their children, and insult our feelings
dy representing us as *talking Apes*, what would they do? But
glory honour and praise to Heaven's King, that the scns and
baughters of Africa, will, in spite of all the opposition of their
enemies, stand forth in all the dignity and glory that is granted
by the Lord to his creature man.

men, and not brutes—the murderers among the
whites would be afraid to show their cruel heads.
But O, my God !—in sorrow I must say it, that my
colour, all over the world, have a mean, servile spirit. They yield in a moment to the whites, let
them be right or wrong—the reason the whites are
able to keep their feet on our throats. Oh ! my
coloured brethren, all over the world, when shall
we arise from this death-like apathy ?—And be men!!
You will notice, if ever we become men (I mean *respectable* men, such as other people are,) we must exert
ourselves to the full. For remember, that it is the
greatest desire and object of the greater part of the
whites, to keep us ignorant, and make us work to
support them and their families.—Here now, in the
Southern and Western Sections of this country.
there are at least three coloured persons for one
white, why is it, that those few weak, good-for-noth-
ing whites, are able to keep so many able men, one
of whom, can put to flight a dozen whites, in wretchedness and misery? It shows at once, what the
blacks are, we are ignorant, abject, servile, and
mean—and the whites know it—they know that we
are too servile to assert our rights as men—or they
would not fool with us as they do. Would they
fool with any other people as they do with us ? No,
they know too well that they would get themselves
ruined. Why do they not bring the inhabitants of
Asia to be body servants to them? They know
they would get their bodies rent and torn from head
to foot. Why do they not get the Aboriginies of this
country to be slaves to them and their children, to
work their farms and dig their mines ? They know
well that the Aboriginies of this country, (or Indians)
would tear them from the earth. The Indians would
not rest day or night, they would be up all times of
night, cutting their cruel throats. But my colour,
(some, not all,) are willing to stand still and be murdered by the cruel whites. In some of the West-
India Islands, and over a large part of South America, there are six or eight coloured persons for one

white. Why do they not take possession of those places? Who hinders them? it is not the avaricious
whites—for they are too busily engaged in laying up
money—derived from the blood and tears of the
blacks. The fact is they are too servile, they
love to have Masters too well!!!!!! Some of our
brethren, too, who seeking more after self aggran-
dizement, than the glory of God, and the welfare of
their brethren, join in with our oppressors, to ridicule and say all manner of evils falsely against our
Bishop. They think, that they are doing great
things, when they get in company with the
whites, to ridicule and make sport of those who are
labouring for their good. Poor ignorant creatures,
they do not know that the sole aim and object of
the whites, are only to make fools and slaves of them
and put the whip to them, and make them work to
support them and their families. But I do say, that
no man can well be a despiser of Bishop Allen, for
his public labors among us, unless he is a despiser
of God and Righteousness. Thus, we see, my
brethren, the two very opposite positions of those
great men, who have written respecting this "Colonizing Plan," (Mr. Clay and his slave holding
party,) men who are resolved to keep us in eternal
wretchedness, are also bent upon sending us to Liberia. While the Reverend Bishop Allen, and his
party, men who have the fear of God, and the welfare of their brethren at heart. The Bishop in par-
ticular, whose labors for the salvation of his brethren, are well known to a large part of those, who
dwell in the United States, are completely opposed
to the plan—and advise us to stay where we are.
Now we have to determine whose advice we will
take respecting this all important matter, whether
we will adhere to Mr. Clay and his slave-holding
party, who have always been our oppressors and
murderers, and who are for colonizing us, more
through apprehension than humanity, or to this godly man who has done so much for our benefit, together with the advice of all the good and wise

among us and the whites. Will any of us leave our
homes and go to Africa? I hope not.* Let them
commence their attack upon us as they did on
our brethren in Ohio, driving and beating us from
our country, and my soul for theirs, they will have
enough of it. Let no man of us budge one step,
and let slave-holders come to beat us from our
country. America is more our country, than it is
the whites—we have enriched it with our *blood and
tears.* The greatest riches in all America have aris-
en from our blood and tears:—and will they drive
us from our property and homes, which we have
earned with our *blood ?* They must look sharp or
this very thing will bring swift destruction upon
them. The Americans have got so fat upon our
blood and groans, that they have almost forgotten
the God of armies. But let them go on.

How cunning slave-holders think they are!!!!—
How much like the king of Egypt, who after he saw
plainly that God was determined to bring out his
people, in spite of him and his, as powerful as
they were. He was willing that Moses, Aaron and
the Elders of Israel, but not all the people should go
and serve the Lord. But God deceived him as he
will christian Americans, unles they are very cau-
tious how they move. What would have become of
the United States of America, was it not for those
among the whites, who not in words barely, but in
truth and in deed, love and fear the Lord Our
Lord and Master said :—† " Whoso shall offend
" one of these little ones which believe in me, it
" were better for him that a millstone were hanged
" about his neck, and that he were drowned in the
" depths of the sea." But the Americans with

---

*Those who are ignorant enough to go to Africa, the coloured
people ought to be glad to have them go, for if they are ignorant
enough to let the whites *fool* them off to Africa, they would be
no small injury to us if they reside in this country.

† See St. Mathew's Gospel, chap. xviii. v. 6.

this very threatening of the Lord's, not only beat his little ones among the Africans, but many of them they put to death or murder. Now the avaricious Americans think that the Lord Jesus Christ will let them off, because his words are no more than the words of a man ! In fact, many of them are so avaricious and ignorant that they do not believe in our Lord and Saviour Jesus Christ. Tyrants may think they are so skilful in State affairs is the reason that the government is preserved. But I tell you, that this country would have been given up long ago, was it not for the lovers of the Lord. They are indeed, the salt of the earth. Remove the people of God among the whites, from this land of blood, and it will stand until they cleverly get out of the way. I adopt the language of the Rev. S. E. Cornish, of N. York, editor of the Rights of All, and say : " Any colored man of common intelligence who gives his countenance and influence to that colony further than its missionary object and interest extend, should be considered as a traitor to his brethren, and discarded by every respectable man of colour: and every member of that society, however pure his motive, whatever may be his religious character and moral worth, should in his efforts to remove the coloured population from their rightful soil, the land of their birth and nativity, be considered as acting gratuitously unrighteous and cruel."

Let me make an appeal brethren, to your hearts, for your cordial co-operation in the circulation of " The Rights of All," among us. The utility of such a vehicle, if rightly conducted, cannot be estimated. I hope that the well informed among us, may see the absolute necessity of their co-operation in its universal spread among us. If we should let it go down, never let us undertake any thing of the kind again, but give up at once and say that we are really so ignorant and wretched that we cannot do any thing at all ! As far as I have seen the writings of its editor, I believe he is not seeking to fill his pockets with money, but has the welfare of his brethren truly at heart. Such men, brethren, ought to be supported by us.

But to return to the colonizing trick. It will be well for me to notice here at once, that I do not mean indiscriminately to condemn all the members and advocates of this scheme, for I believe that there are some friends to the sons of Africa, who are laboring for our salvation, not in words only but in truth and in deed, who have been drawn into this plan. Some, more by persuasion than any thing else; while others, with humane feelings and lively zeal for our good, seeing how much we suffer from the afflictions poured upon us by unmerciful tyrants, are willing to enroll their names in any thing which they think has for its ultimate end our redemption from wretchedness and miseries ; such men, with a heart truly overflowing with gratitude for their past services and zeal in our cause, I humbly beg to examine this plot minutely, and see if the end which they have in view will be completely consummated by such a course of procedure. Our friends who have been imperceptibly drawn into this plot I view with tenderness, and would not for the world injure their feelings, and I have only to hope for the future, that they will withdraw themselves from it; for I declare to them, that the plot is not for the glory of God, but on the contrary the perpetuation of slavery in this country, which will ruin them and the country forever, unless something is immediately done.

Do the colonizationists think to send us off without first being reconciled to us ? Do they think to bundle us up like brutes and send us off, as they did our brethren of the State of Ohio ? Have they not to be reconciled to us, or reconcile us to them, for the cruelties with which they have afflicted our fathers and us ? Methinks colonizationists think they have a set of brutes to deal with, sure enough. Do they think to drive us from our country and homes, after having enriched it with our blood and tears, and keep back millions of our dear brethren, sunk in the

most barbarous wretchedness, to dig up gold and
silver for them and their children ? Surely, the
Americans must think that we are brutes, as some
of them have represented us to be. They think that
we do not feel for our brethren, whom they are murdering by the inches, but they are dreadfully deceived. I acknowledge that there are some deceitful and hypocritical wretches among us, who will
tell us one thing while they mean another, and thus
they go on aiding our enemies to oppress themselves
and us. But I declare this day before my Lord and
Master, that I believe there are some true-hearted
sons of Africa, in this land of oppression, but pretended *liberty* ! ! ! ! !—who do in reality feel for their
suffering brethren, who are held in bondage by tyrants. Some of the advocates of this cunningly de-
vised plot of Satan represent us to be the greatest
set of cut throats in the world, as though God, wants
us to take his work out of his hand before he is ready.
Does not vengeance belong to the Lord ? Is he
not able to repay the Americans for their cruelties,
with which they have afflicted Africa's sons and
daughters, without our interference, unless we are
ordered ? Is it surprising to think that the Americans, having the bible in their hands, do not believe
it. Are not the hearts of all men in the hands of
the God of battles ? And does he not suffer some,
in consequence of cruelties, to go on until they are
irrecoverably lost ? Now, what can be more aggravating, than for the Americans, after having treated
us so bad, to hold us up to the world as such great
throat cutters ? It appears to me as though they
are resolved to assail us with every species of afflic-
tion that their ingenuity can invent. (☞ See the
African Repository and Colonial Journal, from its
commencement to the present day—see how we are,
through the medium of that periodical, abused and
held up by the Americans, as the greatest nuisance
to society, and throat-cutters in the world.) But the
Lord sees their actions. Americans ! notwithstanding you have and do continue to treat us more cruel

than any heathen nation ever did a people it had subjected to the same condition that you have us. Now
let us reason—I mean you of the United States,
whom I believe God designs to save from destruc-
tiom, if you will hear. For I declare to you, whether
you believe it or not, that there are some on the continent of America, who will never be able to repent.
God will surely destroy them, to show you his disapprobation of the murders they and you have inflicted on us. I say, let us reason ; had you not better take our body, while you have it in your power,
and while we are yet ignorant and wretched, not
knowing but a little, give us education, and teach us
the pure religion of our Lord and Master, which is
calculated to make the lion lay down in peace with the
lamb, and which millions of you have beaten us
nearly to death for trying to obtain since we have
been among you, and thus, at once, gain our affection,
while we are ignorant ? Remember Americans, that
we must and shall be free, and enlightened as you
are, will you wait until we shall, under God, obtain
our lib erty by the crushing arm of power ? Will it
not be dreadful for you ? I speak Americans for your
good. We must and shall be free I say, in spite of
you. You may do your best to keep us in wretchedness and misery, to enrich you and your children
but God will deliver us from under you. And wo,
wo, will be to you if we have to obtain our freedom by fighting. Throw away your fears and prejudices then, and enlighten us and treat us like
men, and we will like you more than we do now hate
you,*and tell us now no more about colonization, for
America is as much our country, as it is yours.—
Treat us like men, and there is no danger but we
will all live in peace and happiness together. For
we are not like you, hard hearted, unmerciful, and
unforgiving. What a happy country this will be, if
the whites will listen. What nation under heaven,
will be able to do any thing with us, unless God gives

---

*You are not astonished at my saying we hate you, for if we are
men, we cannot but hate you, while you are treating us like dogs.

us up into his hand ? But Americans, I declare to
you, while you keep us and our children in bondage,
and treat us like brutes, to make us support you and
your families, we cannot be your friends. You do
not look for it, do you? Treat us then like men,
and we will be your friends. And there is not a
doubt in my mind, but that the whole of the past
will be sunk into oblivion, and we yet, under God,
will become a united and happy people. The whites
may say it is impossible, but remember that nothing
is impossible with God.

The Americans may say or do as they please, but
they have to raise us from the condition of brutes
to that of respectable men, and to make a national
acknowledgement to us for the wrongs they have
inflicted on us. As unexpected, strange, and wild
as these propositions may to some appear, it is no
less a fact, that unless they are complied with, the
Americans of the United States, though they may
for a little while escape, God will yet weigh them
in a balance, and if they are not superior to other
men, as they have represented themselves to be, he
will give them wretchedness to their very heart's
content.

And now brethren, having concluded these four
Articles, I submit them, together with my Preamble,
dedicated to the Lord for your inspection, in language so very simple, that the most ignorant, who
can read at all, may easily understand—of which
you may make the best you possibly can.* Should

---

*Some of my brethren, who are sensible, do not take an interest
in enlightening the minds of our more ignorant brethren respecting this *Book*, and in reading it to them, just as though they will
not have either to rise or fall by what is written in this book. Do
they believe that I would be so foolish as to put out a book of this
kind, without strict—ah ! very strict commandments of the Lord ?
—Surely the blacks and whites must think that I am ignorant
enough. Do they think that I would have the audacious wickedness to take the name of my God in vain ?
   Notice, I said in the concluding clause of Article 3--I call God,
I call Angels, I call men to witness, that the destruction of the
Americans is at hand, and will be speedily consumated unless they
repent. Now I wonder if the world think that I would take the

tyrants take it into their heads to emancipate any of
you, remember that your freedom is yonr natural
right. You are men, as well as they, and instead
of returning thanks to them for your freedom, return it to the Holy Ghost, who is your rightful owner.
If they do not want to part with your labours, which
have enriched them, let them keep you, and my word
for it, that God Almighty, will break their strong
band. Do you believe this my brethren ?—See my
Address delivered before the General Coloured
Association of Massachusetts, which may be found
in Freedom's Journal, for Dec. 20, 1828.—See the
last clause of that Address. Whether you believe
it or not, I tell you that God will dash tyrants, in
combination with devils, into atoms, and will bring
you out from your wretchedness and miseries,
under these *Christian People! ! ! ! !*

Those philanthropists and lovers of the human
family, who have volunteered their services for our
redemption from wretchedness, have a high claim
on our gratitude, and we should always view them
as our greatest earthly benefactors.

If any are anxious to ascertain who I am, know
the world, that I am one of the oppressed, degraded
and wretched sons of Africa, rendered so by the
avaricious and unmerciful, among the whites.—If
any wish to plunge me into the wretched incapaci-
ty of a slave, or murder me for the truth, know ye,
that I am in the hand of God, and at your disposal.
I count my life not dear unto me, but I am ready
to be offered at any moment. For what is the use
of living when in fact I am dead. But remember,
Americans, that as miserable, wretched, degraded
and abject as you have made us in preceding, and
in this generation, to support you and your families,
that some of you (whites) on the continent of Amer-

name of God in this way in vain ? What do they think I take God
to be ? Do they suppose that I would trifle with that God who will
not have his holy name taken in vain ?—He will show you and the
world, in due time, whether this book is for his glory, or written by
me through envy to the whites, as some have represented.

ica, will yet curse the day that you ever were born. You want slaves, and want us for your slaves ! !!   My colour will yet, root some of you out of the very face of the earth !! ! ! !! You may doubt it if you please.   I know that thousands will doubt—they think they have us so well secured in wretchedness, to them and their children, that it is impossible for such things to occur.   So did the antideluvians doubt Noah, until the day in which the flood came and swept them away.   So did the Sodomites doubt, until Lot had got out of the City, and God rained down fire and brimstone from heaven, upon them and burnt them up.   So did the king of Egypt doubt the very existence of a God, he said, "who is the Lord, that I should let Israel go ?"   Did he not find to his sorrow, who the Lord was, when he and all his mighty men of war, were smothered to death in the Red Sea ?— So did the Romans doubt, many of them were really so ignorant, that they thought the world of mankind were made to be slaves to them ; just as many of the Americans think now, of my colour.— But they got dreadfully deceived.   When men got their eyes opened, they made the murderers scamper. The way in which they cut their tyrannical throats, was not much inferior to the way the Romans or murderers, served them, when they held them in wretchedness and degradation under their feet.   So would Christian Americans doubt, if God should send an Angel from heaven to preach their funeral sermon.   The fact is, the christians having a name to live, while they are dead, think that God will screen them on that ground.

See the hundreds and thousands of us that are thrown into the seas by Christians, and murdered by them in other ways.   They cram us into their vessel holds in chains and in hand-cuffs—men, women and children, all together !!   O! save us, we pray thee, thou God of heaven and of earth, from the devouring hands of the white Christians !! ! !!!

Oh! thou Alpha and Omega!
The beginning and the end,
Enthron'd thou art, in Heaven above,
Surrounded by angels there:

From whence thou seest the miseries
To which we are subject;
The whites have murder'd us, O God!
And kept us ignorant of thee.

Not satisfied with this, my Lord!
They throw us in the seas:
Be pleas'd, we pray, for Jesus' sake,
To save us from their grasp.

We believe that, for thy glory's sake,
Thou wilt deliver us;
But that thou may'st effect these things,
Thy glory must be sought.

———•———

In conclusion, I ask the candid and unprejudiced of the whole world, to search the pages of historians diligently, and see if the Antediluvians—the Sodomites—the Egyptians—the Babylonians—the Ninevites—the Carthagenians—the Persians—the Macedonians—the Greeks—the Romans—the Mahometans—the Jews---or devils, ever treated a set of human beings, as the white Christians of America do us, the blacks, or Africans.---I also ask the attention of the world of mankind to the declaration of these very American people, of the United States.

———

A Declaration made July 4, 1776.

It says, *"When in the course of human events,
" it becomes necessary for one people to dissolve
" the political bands which have connected them
" with another, and to assume among the Powers of
" the earth, the separate and equal station to which
" the laws of nature and of nature's God entitle

———

*See the Declaration of Independence of the United States.

" them, a decent respect for the opinions of mankind
" requires that they should declare the causes which
" impel them to the separation.   We hold these
" truths to be self evident, that all men are created
" equal, that they are endowed by their Creator
" with certain unalienable rights ; that among these
" are life, liberty, and the pursuit of happiness ; that
" to secure these rights, governments are instituted
" among men, deriving their just powers from the
" consent of the governed ; that whenever any form
" of government becomes destructive of these ends it
" is the right of the people to alter or to abolish it,
" and to institute a new government laying its
" foundation on such principles, and organizing its
" powers in such form as to them shall seem most
" likely to effect their safety and happiness.   Pru-
" dence, indeed, will dictate that governments long
" established should not be changed for light and
" transient causes ; and accordingly all experience
" hath shewn, that mankind are more disposed to
" suffer, while evils are sufferable, than to right
" themselves by abolishing the forms to which they
" are accustomed.   But when a long train of abuses
" and usurpations, pursuing invariably the same ob-
" ject, evinces a design to reduce them under abso-
" lute despotism, it is their right, it is their duty to
" throw off such government, and to provide new
" guards for their future security."   See your declaration, Americans ! !   Do you understand your
own language ?   Hear your language, proclaim-
ed to the world, July 4, 1776—☞" We hold
" these truths to be self evident—that *ALL* MEN
" ARE CREATED EQUAL !   *that they are endowed*
" *by their Creator with certain unalienable rights ;*
" *that among these are life, liberty, and the pursuit*
" *of happiness ! !"*   Compare your own language
above, extracted from your Declaration of Independence, with your cruelties and murders inflicted by your cruel and unmerciful fathers on
ourselves on our fathers and on us, men who have

never given your fathers or you the least provocation ! ! !

Hear your language further ! ☞ "But when a "long train of abuses and usurpations, pursuing "invariably the same object, evinces a design to re-"duce them under absolute despotism, it is their "*right*, it is their *duty*, to throw off such govern-"ment, and to provide new guards for their future "security."

Now, Americans ! I ask you candidly, was your sufferings under Great Britain one hundredth part as cruel and tyrannical as you have rendered ours under you ? Some of you, no doubt, believe that we will never throw off your murderous government, and " provide .new guards for our future " security." If Satan has made you believe it, will he not deceive you ?* Do the whites say, I being a black man, ought to be humble, which I readily admit ? I ask them, ought they not to be as humble as I ? or do they think they can measure arms with Jehovah ? Will not the Lord yet humble them ? or will not these very coloured people, whom they now treat worse than brutes, yet under God, humble them low down enough ? Some of the whites are ignorant enough to tell us, that we ought to be submissive to them, that they may keep their feet on our throats. And if we do not submit to be beaten to death by them, we are bad creatures and of course must be damned, &c. If any man wishes to hear this doctrine openly preached to us by the American preachers, let him go into the Southern and Western sections of this country—I do not speak from hearsay—what I have written, is what I have seen and heard myself. No man may think that my book is made up of conjecture—I have travelled and observed nearly the whole of those things myself, and what little I did not get by

---

*The Lord has not taught the Americans that we will not some day or other throw off their chains and hand-cuffs, from our hands and feet, and their devilish lashes (which some of them shall have enough of yet) from off our backs.

my own observation, I received from those among the whites and blacks, in whom the greatest confidence may be placed.

The Americans may be as vigilant as they please, but they cannot be vigilant enough for the Lord, neither can they hide themselves, where he will not find and bring them out.

1 Thy presence why withdraw'st thou, Lord?
    Why hid'st thou now thy face,
  When dismal times of deep distress
    Call for thy wonted grace?

2 The wicked, swell'd with lawless pride,
    Have made the poor their prey;
  O let them fall by those designs
    Which they for others lay.

3 For straight they triumph, if success
    Their thriving crimes attend;
  And sordid wretches, whom God hates,
    Perversely they commend.

4 To own a pow'r above themselves
    Their haughty pride disdains;
  And, therefore, in their stubborn mind
    No thought of God remains.

5 Oppressive methods they pursue,
    And all their foes they slight;
  Because thy judgements, unobserv'd,
    Are far above their sight.

6 They fondly think their prosp'rous state
    Shall unmolested be;
  They think their vain designs shall thrive,
    From all misfortune free.

7 Vain and deceitful is their speech,
    With curses fill'd, and lies;
  By which the mischief of their heart
    They study to disguise.

8 Near public roads they lie conceal'd,
    And all their art employ,
  The innocent and poor at once
    To rifle and destroy.

9 Not lions crouching in their dens,
    Surprise their heedless prey
  With greater cunning, or express
    More savage rage than they.

10 Sometimes they act the harmless man,
   And modest looks they wear;
   That so, deceiv'd, the poor may less
   Their sudden onset fear

PART II.

11 For God, they think, no notice takes
   Of their unrighteous deeds;
   He never minds the suff'ring poor,
   Nor their oppression heeds.

12 But thou, O Lord, at length arise,
   Stretch forth thy mighty arm,
   And by the greatness of thy pow'r,
   Defend the poor from harm.

13 No longer let the wicked vaunt,
   And, proudly boasting, say,
   " Tush, God regards not what we do;
   " He never will repay."—*Common Prayer Book.*

---

1 Shall I for fear of feeble man,
   The Spirit's course in me restrain?
   Or, undismay'd in deed and word.
   Be a true witness of my Lord.

2 Aw'd by mortal's frown shall I
   Conceal the word of God Most High!
   How then before thee shall I dare
   To stand, or how thine anger bear?

3 Shall I, to sooth th' unholy throng,
   Soften the truth, or smooth my tongue,
   To gain earth's gilded toys, or flee
   The cross endur'd, my Lord, by thee?

4 What then is he whose scorn I dread?
   Whose wrath or hate makes me afraid
   A man! an heir of death! a slave
   To sin! a bubble on the wave!

5 Yea, let men rage: since thou wilt spread
   Thy shadowing wings around my head:
   Since in all pain thy tender love
   Will still my sure refreshment prove.

                             Wesley's Collection.

AN ADDRESS

TO THE SLAVES OF THE UNITED STATES OF AMERICA.

(REJECTED BY THE NATIONAL CONVENTION, 1843.)

BY HENRY HIGHLAND GARNET.

PREFACE.

The following Address was first read at the National Convention held at Buffalo, N. Y., in 1843.   Since that time it has been slightly modified, retaining, however, all of its original doctrine. The document elicited more discussion than any other paper that was ever brought before that, or any other deliberative body of colored persons, and their friends.   Gentlemen who opposed the Address, based their objections on these grounds. 1. That the document was war-like, and encouraged insurrection ; and 2. That if the Convention should adopt it, that those delegates who lived near the borders of the slave states, would not dare to return to their homes.   The Address was rejected by a small majority ; and now in compliance with the earnest reqrest of many who heard it, and in conformity to the wishes of numerous friends who are anxious to see it, the author now gives it to the public, praying God that this little book may be borne on the four winds of heaven, until the principles it contains shall be understood and adopted by every slave in the Union.   H. H. G.

Troy, N. Y., April 15, 1848.

ADDRESS TO THE SLAVES OF THE U. S.

Brethren and Fellow Citizens:

Your brethren of the north, east, and west have been accustomed to meet together in National Conventions, to sympathize with each other, and to weep over your unhappy condition. In these meetings we have addressed all classes of the free, but we have never until this time, sent a word of consolation and advice to you. We have been contented in sitting still and mourning over your sorrows, earnestly hoping that before this day, your sacred liberties would have been restored. But, we have hoped in vain. Years have rolled on, and tens of thousands have been borne on streams of blood, and tears, to the shores of eternity. While you have been oppressed, we have also been partakers with you; nor can we be free while you are enslaved. We therefore write to you as being bound with you.

Many of you are bound to us, not only by the ties of a common humanity, but we are connected by the more tender relations of parents, wives, husbands, children, brothers, and sisters, and friends. As such we most affectionately address you.

Slavery has fixed a deep gulf between you and us, and while it shuts out from you the relief and consolation which your friends would willingly render, it afflicts and persecutes you with a fierceness which we might not expect to see in the fiends of hell. But still the Almighty Father of Mercies has left to us a glimmering ray of hope, which shines out like a lone star in a cloudy sky. Mankind are becoming wiser, and better—the oppressor's power is fading. and you, every day, are becoming better informed, and more nu_merous. Your grievances, brethren, are many. We shall not attempt, in this short address, to present to the world, all the dark catalogue of this nation's sins, which have been committed upon an innocent people. Nor is it indeed, necessary, for you feel them from day to day, and all the civilized world look upon them with amazement.

Two hundred and twenty-seven years ago, the first of our injured race were brought to the shores of America. They came not with glad spirits to select their homes, in the New World. They came not with their own consent, to find an unmolested enjoyment of the blessings of this fruitful soil. The first dealings which they had with those calling themselves Christians, exhibited to them the worst features of corrupt and sordid hearts; and convinced them that no cruelty is too great, no villainy, and no robbery too abhorrent for even enlightened men to perform, when influenced by avarice, and lust. Neither did they come flying upon the wings of Liberty, to a land of freedom. But, they came with broken hearts, from their beloved native land, and were doomed to unrequited toil, and deep degradation. Nor did the evil of their bondage end at their emancipation by death. Succeeding generations inherited their chains, and millions have come from eternity into time, and have returned again to the world of spirits, cursed, and ruined by American Slavery.

The propagators of the system, or their immediate ancestors very soon discovered its growing evil, and its tremendous wickedness, and secret promises were made to destroy it. The gross inconsistency of a people holding slaves, who had themselves " ferried o'er the wave," for freedom's sake, was too apparent to be entirely overlooked. The voice of Freedom cried, " emancipate your Slaves." Humanity supplicated with tears, for the deliverance of the children of Africa. Wisdom urged her solemn plea. The bleeding captive plead his innocence, and pointed to Christianity who stood weeping at the cross. Jehovah frowned upon the nefarious institution, and thunderbolts, red with vengeance, struggled to leap forth to blast the guilty wretches who maintained it. But all was vain. Slavery had stretched its dark wings of death over the land, the Church stood silently by—the priests prophesied falsely, and the people loved to have it so. Its throne is established, and now it reigns triumphantly.

Nearly three millions of your fellow citizens, are prohibited by law, and public opinion, (which in this country is stronger than law), from reading the Book of Life. Your intellect has been destroyed as much as possible, and every ray of light they have attempted to shut out from your minds. The oppressors themselves have become involved in the ruin. They have become weak, sensual, and rapacious. They have cursed you—they have cursed themselves—they have cursed the earth which they have trod. In the language of a Southern statesman, we can truly say, " even the wolf, driven back long since by the approach of man, now returns after the lapse of a hundred years, and howls amid the desolations of slavery."

The colonists threw the blame upon England. They said that the mother country entailed the evil upon them, and that they would rid themselves of it if they·could. The world thought they were sincere, and the philanthropic pitied them. But time soon tested

their sincerity. In a few years, the colonists grew strong ....
severed themselves from the British Government. Their Indepen
dence was declared, and they took their station among the sovereign powers of the earth. The declaration was a glorious document. Sages admired it, and the patriotic of every nation rever-
enced the Godlike sentiments which it contained. When the
power of Government returned to their hands, did they emancipate
the slaves? No; they rather added new links to our chains.
Were they ignorant of the principles of Liberty? Certainly they
were not. The sentiments of their revolutionary orators fell in
burning eloquence upon their hearts, and with one voice they cried,
LIBERTY OR DEATH. O, what a sentence was that! It ran from
soul to soul like electric fire, and nerved the arm of thousands to
fight in the holy cause of Freedom. Among the diversity of opinions that are entertained in regard to physical resistance, there are
but a few found to gainsay that stern declaration. We are among
those who do not.

SLAVERY! How much misery is comprehended in that single word. What mind is there that does not shrink from its
direful effects? Unless the image of God is obliterated from the
soul, all men cherish the love of Liberty. The nice discerning
political economist does not regard the sacred right, more than the
untutored African who roams in the wilds of Congo. Nor has the
one more right to the full enjoyment of his freedom than the other.
In every man's mind the good seeds of liberty are planted, and he
who brings his fellow down so low, as to make him contented with
a condition of slavery, commits the highest crime against God and
man. Brethren, your oppressors aim to do this. They endeavor to
make you as much like brutes as possible. When they have
blinded the eyes of your mind—when they have embittered the
sweet waters of life—when they have shut out the light which
shines from the word of God—then, and not till then has American slavery done its perfect work.

TO SUCH DEGRADATION IT IS SINFUL IN THE EXTREME FOR YOU TO
MAKE VOLUNTARY SUBMISSION. The divine commandments, you
are in duty bound to reverence, and obey. If you do not obey
them you will surely meet with the displeasure of the Almighty
He requires you to love him supremely, and your neighbor as
yourself—to keep the Sabbath day holy—to search the Scriptures
—and bring up your children with respect for his laws, and to
worship no other God but him. But slavery sets all these at naught'

and hurls defiance in the face of Jehovah. The forlorn condition in which you are placed does not destroy your moral obligation to God. You are *not* certain of Heaven, because you suffer yourselves to remain in a state of slavery, where you cannot obey the commandments of the Sovereign of the universe. If the ignorance of slavery is a passport to heaven, then it is a blessing, and no curse, and you should rather desire its perpetuity than its abolition. God will not receive slavery, nor ignorance, nor any other state of mind, for love, and obedience to him. Your condition does not absolve you from your moral obligation. The diabolical injustice by which your liberties are cloven down, NEITHER GOD, NOR ANGELS, OR JUST MEN, COMMAND YOU TO SUFFER FOR A SINGLE MOMENT. THEREFORE IT IS YOUR SOLEMN AND IMPERATIVE DUTY TO USE EVERY MEANS, BOTH MORAL, INTELLECTUAL, AND PHYSICAL, THAT PROMISE SUCCESS. If a band of heathen men should attempt to enslave a race of Christians, and to place their children under the influence of some false religion, surely, heaven would frown upon the men who would not resist such aggression, even to death. If, on the other hand, a band of Christians should attempt to enslave a race of heathen men and to entail slavery upon them, and to keep them in heathenism in the midst of Christianity, the God of heaven would smile upon every effort which the injured might make to disenthral themselves.

Brethren, it is as wrong for your lordly oppressors to keep you in slavery, as it was for the man thief to steal our ancestors from the coast of Africa. You should therefore now use the same manner of resistance, as would have been just in our ancestors, when the bloody foot prints of the first remorseless soul thief was placed upon the shores of our fatherland. The humblest peasant is as free in the sight of God, as the proudest monarch that ever swayed a sceptre. Liberty is a spirit sent out from God, and like its great Author, is no respecter of persons.

Brethren, the time has come when you must act for yourselves. It is an old and true saying, that "if hereditary bondmen would be free, they must themselves strike the blow." You can plead your own cause, and do the work of emancipation better than any others. The nations of the old world are moving in the great cause of universal freedom, and some of them at least, will ere long, do you justice. The combined powers of Europe have placed their broad seal of disapprobation upon the African slave trade. But in the slave holding parts of the United States, the trade is as brisk as ev-

er. They buy and sell you as though you were brute beasts. The
North has done much—her opinion of slavery in the abstract is
known. But in regard to the South, we adopt he opinion of the
New York Evangelist—" We have advanced so far, that the cause
apparently waits for a more effectual door to be thrown open than
has been yet." We are about to point you to that more effectual
door. Look around you, and behold the bosoms of your loving
wives, heaving with untold agonies! Hear the cries of your poor
children! Remember the stripes your fathers bore. Think of
the torture and disgrace of your noble mothers. Think of your
wretched sisters, loving virtue and purity, as they are driven into
concubinage, and are exposed to the unbridled lusts of incarnate devils. Think of the undying glory that hangs around the ancient
name of Africa :—and forget not that you are native-born American citizens, and as such, you are justly entitled to all the rights
that are granted to the freest. Think how many tears you have
poured out upon the soil which you have cultivated with unrequited toil, ana enriched with your blood ; and then go to your lordly
enslavers, and tell them plainly, that YOU ARE DETERMINED TO BE
FREE. Appeal to their sense of justice, and tell them that they
have no more right to oppress you, than you have to enslave them.
Entreat them to remove the grievous burdens which they have im-
posed upon you, and to remunerate you for your labor. Promise
them renewed diligence in the cultivation of the soil, if they will
render to you an equivalent for your services. Point them to the
increase of happiness and prosperity in the British West Indies,
since the act of Emancipation. Tell them in language which
they cannot misunderstand, of the exceeding sinfulness of slavery,
and of a future judgment, and of the righteous retributions of an indignant God. Inform them that all you desire, is FREEDOM, and
that nothing else will suffice. Do this, and for ever after cease to
toil for the heartless tyrants, who give you no other reward but
stripes and abuse. If they then commence the work of death,
they, and not you, will be responsible for the consequences. You
had far better all die—*die immediately*, than live slaves, and entail
your wretchedness upon your posterity. If you would be free in
this generation, here is your only hope. However much you and
all of us may desire it, there is not much hope of Redemption without the shedding of blood. If you must bleed, let it all come at
once—rather, *die freemen, than live to be slaves.* It is impossible,
like the children of Israel, to make a grand Exodus from the land
of bondage. THE PHARAOHS ARE ON BOTH SIDES OF THE BLOOD-

RED WATERS! You cannot remove en masse, to the dominions of the British Queen—nor can you pass through Florida, and over-run Texas, and at last find peace in Mexico. The propagators of American slavery are spending their blood and treasure, that they may plant the black flag in the heart of Mexico, and riot in the halls of the Montezumas. In the language of the Rev. Robert Hall, when addressing the volunteers of Bristol, who were rushing forth to repel the invasion of Napoleon, who threatened to lay waste the fair homes of England, " Religion is too much interested in your behalf, not to shed over you her most gracious influences."

You will not be compelled to spend much time in order to become inured to hardships. From the first moment that you breathed the air of heaven, you have been accustomed to nothing else but hardships. The heroes of the American Revolution were never put upon harder fare, than a peck of corn, and a few herrings per week. You have not become enervated by the luxuries of life. Your sternest energies have been beaten out upon the anvil of severe trial. Slavery has done this, to make you sub-servient to its own purposes ; but it has done more than this, it has prepared you for any emergency. If you receive good treatment, it is what you could hardly expect ; if you meet with pain, sorrow, and even death, these are the common lot of the slaves.

Fellow-men! patient sufferers ! behold your dearest rights crushed to the earth ! See your sons murdered, and your wives, mothers, and sisters, doomed to prostitution ! In the name of the merciful God ! and by all that life is worth, let it no longer be a debateable question, whether it is better to choose LIBERTY or DEATH !

In 1822, Denmark Veazie, of South Carolina, formed a plan for the liberation of his fellow men. In the whole history of human efforts to overthrow slavery, a more complicated and tremendous plan was never formed. He was betrayed by the treachery of his own people, and died a martyr to freedom. Many a brave hero fell, but History, faithful to her high trust, will transcribe his name on the same monument with Moses, Hampden, Tell, Bruce, and Wallace, Touissaint L'Overteur, Lafayette and Washington. That tremendous movement shook the whole empire of slavery. The guilty soul thieves were overwhelmed with fear. It is a matter of fact, that at that time, and in consequence of the threatened revolution, the slave states talked strongly of emancipation. But they blew but one blast of the trumpet of freedom, and then laid it aside As these men became quiet, the slaveholders ceased to talk about emancipation : and now, behold your condition to-day ! Angels sigh over it, and humanity has long since exhausted her tears in weeping on your account!

The patriotic Nathaniel Turner followed Denmark Veazie. He was goaded to desperation by wrong and injustice. By Despotism, his name has been recorded on the list of infamy, but future generations will number him among the noble and brave.

Next arose the immortal Joseph Cinque, the hero of the Amistad. He was a native African, and by the help of God he emancipated a whole ship-load of his fellow men on the high seas. And he now sings of liberty on the sunny hills of Africa, and beneath his native palm trees, where he hears the lion roar, and feels himself as free as that king of the forest. Next arose Madison Washington, that bright star of freedom, and took his station in the constellation of freedom. He was a slave on board the brig Creole, of Richmond, bound to New Orleans, that great slave mart, with a hundred and four others. Nineteen struck for liberty or death. But one life was taken, and the whole were emancipated, and the vessel was carried into Nassau, New Providence. Noble men! Those who have fallen in freedom's conflict, their memories will be cherished by the true hearted, and the God-fearing, in all future generations; those who are living, their names are surrounded by a halo of glory.

We do not advise you to attempt a revolution with the sword, because it would be INEXPEDIENT. Your numbers are too small, and moreover the rising spirit of the age, and the spirit of the gospel, are opposed to war and bloodshed. But from this moment cease to labor for tyrants who will not remunerate you. Let every slave throughout the land do this, and the days of slavery are numbered. You cannot be more oppressed than you have been— you cannot suffer greater cruelties than you have already. RATHER DIE FREEMEN, THAN LIVE TO BE SLAVES. Remember that you are THREE MILLIONS.

It is in your power so to torment the God-cursed slaveholders, that they will be glad to let you go free. If the scale was turned and black men were the masters, and white men the slaves, every destructive agent and element would be employed to lay the oppressor low. Danger and death would hang over their heads day and night. Yes, the tyrants would meet with plagues more terrible than those of Pharaoh. But you are a patient people. You act as though you were made for the special use of these devils. You act as though your daughters were born to pamper the lusts of your masters and overseers. And worse than all, you tamely submit, while your lords tear your wives from your embraces, and defile them before your eyes. In the name of God we ask, are you men? Where is the blood of your fathers? Has it all run out of your veins? Awake, awake; millions of voices are calling you! Your dead fathers speak to you from their graves. Heaven, as with a voice of thunder, calls on you to arise from the dust.

Let your motto be RESISTANCE! RESISTANCE! RESISTANCE!— No oppressed people have ever secured their liberty without resistance. What kind of resistance you had better make, you must decide by the circumstances that surround you, and according to the suggestion of expediency. Brethren, adieu. Trust in the living God. Labor for the peace of the human race, and remember that you are three millions.